MAN EATE
JUNGLE K

Kenneth Anderson (1910-1974) was a hunter, nature enthusiast and chronicler of wildlife. His hunting expeditions involved several close encounters with man-eating tigers, rogue elephants, leopards and other wild animals. He wrote about eight books and sixty short stories which recount many of his real-life adventures and hunting exploits in the jungles of South India. In 2000, his collected works, *The Kenneth Anderson Omnibus*, were published in two volumes.

He spent most of his life in Bangalore, where he was employed with an aeronautics company. Anderson's invaluable contribution to shikar literature in India continues to inspire scores of wildlife lovers.

Visit www.facebook.com/groups/kennethanderson to know more about the author.

By the same author

Tales from the Indian Jungle
The Call of the Man-Eater
The Black Panther of Sivanipalli
The Tiger Roars
Jungles Long Ago

KENNETH ANDERSON
MAN EATERS AND JUNGLE KILLERS

RUPA

Published by
Rupa Publications India Pvt. Ltd 2002
7/16, Ansari Road, Daryaganj
New Delhi 110002

Sales centres:
Allahabad Bengaluru Chennai
Hyderabad Jaipur Kathmandu
Kolkata Mumbai

Edition copyright © Rupa Publications India Pvt. Ltd 2002

The views and opinions expressed in this book are the author's own and the facts are as reported by him/her which have been verified to the extent possible, and the publishers are not in any way liable for the same.

All rights reserved.
No part of this publication may be reproduced, transmitted, or stored in a retrieval system, in any form or by any means, electronic, mechanical, photocopying, recording or otherwise, without the prior permission of the publisher.

ISBN: 978-81-716-7563-0

Fifth impression 2018

10 9 8 7 6 5

The moral right of the author has been asserted.

Printed at Gopsons Papers Ltd, Noida

This book is sold subject to the condition that it shall not, by way of trade or otherwise, be lent, resold, hired out, or otherwise circulated, without the publisher's prior consent, in any form of binding or cover other than that in which it is published.

Contents

Introduction	vii
The Marauder of Kempekarai	1
Alam Bux and the Big Black Bear	38
The Mamandur Man-Eater	53
The Crossed-Tusker of Gerhetti	73
The Sangam Panther	95
The Ramapuram Tiger	117
The Great Panther of Mudiyanoor	136
The Mauler of Rajnagara	151

Introduction

TIME AND CIVILISATION MARCH INEXORABLY ONWARD, BRINGING IN their wake industrialisation, higher standards of living, and greater amenities and comforts, but at the price, it seems, of an ever-diminishing appreciation of Nature. Her face has been scarred and furrowed by man-made projects and constructions. Every minute of the day hoary trees, the giants of the forest, some of them centuries old, crash to earth, felled by the hand of man, either for the sake of the timber they provide or to make room for the constant expansion of a mechanical culture: a condition in which only a few are happy and which is occasionally punctuated by the most barbaric atrocities.

With the crash of the forest giants, other things take their departure too: the wild animals, the birds and all the living creatures that once beautified our lands. They are all disappearing, and very rapidly too!

Such was the case long ago with the American prairies, once the home of countless bison and now completely cleared of its ancient tenants. Africa is rapidly following suit. Where

INTRODUCTION

are those myriad heads of game that once covered the face of that wonderful land? Some still remain; but long ago the bones of the vast majority lay bleaching in the hot African sun, scattered across those thousands of miles by the bullets of avaricious, unscrupulous and money-making hunters—men who sometimes shot the mighty elephant for commercial ends, literally by thousands.

India, too, has lost much, for the decrease in the variety and number of her wild life has been alarming. I know localities where until 1930 the moaning sough of a tiger or the guttural sawing of the panther were normal sounds in the night, followed always by the warning call of sambar and other members of the deer family. Now the night passes without a sound, except perhaps for a persistently chirping cricket. Where once the pug-marks of a tiger and other wild-animal trails would tell their morning story of the creatures that had passed that way during the night, the tiny tracks of a few rabbits might today indicate that they at least have not been exterminated.

I do not wish to enter into argument as to how and why a country loses so much with the disappearance of her wild life. Anyone who has never come to know and love the jungle, its solitude and all that its denizens signify, could never appreciate such sentiments, nor the sense of irreparable loss and sorrow felt by those who look for the once familiar forms that are no longer there, or listen vainly for those once familiar sounds that were music to their ears, only to be greeted by a devastating silence.

One cannot doubt that the time will come when even the few living creatures that today remain in their natural state will have vanished, and man may then, and only then, realise too late what a priceless asset he has wantonly allowed to be thrown away.

INTRODUCTION

I write these stories not only in the hope that they may afford some degree of pleasure to the adventurous, but that they may also indicate what the conditions of living, in and near the great forests of India, were once like, and to show too that one of the greatest opportunities that any individual could desire, of showing his skill and perseverance in the fine sport of 'Shikar', is now in the process of vanishing forever.

One

The Marauder of Kempekarai

IF YOU TRY TO IMAGINE TWO PARALLEL RANGES OF LOFTY HILLS, averaging four thousand feet and more above the sea, with a valley between them about five miles across, covered with dense forest except for the craggy summits, you will have in your mind's eye the background of my story. It is set in the North Salem district of the Presidency of Madras in southern India.

The hills run from north to south, and the easterly range is the more lofty of the two, culminating at its southern point in the peak of Gutherayan, which is over 4,500 feet high. On its slopes stands a lovely little forest lodge, known as Kodekarai Bungalow, amidst some of the finest scenery in the world. Rolling hills and jutting cliffs are to be seen in every direction. The sun rises in shades of rose-pink above the billowing clouds of morning mist, to set eventually in the orange-bronze reflections behind the western range. Then the moon comes up in pallid splendour, tipping the hill-tops, and later the deep valleys, with her luminous wand. Through the night she rides the heavens, silent witness of many a jungle tragedy in the dark forests below. The scream of a dying sambar or the shrill shriek of a spotted stag have often gone forth in vain to that same full moon as they spilled their life-blood on the forest floor beneath the paws of a hungry tiger.

More than twenty years ago I had the honour of meeting the brother of King Amanuallah of Afghanistan, who was exiled from his native country and lived at Kodekarai Bungalow, which was his favourite abode. He told me that he loved the place, that its scenery reminded him of his beloved Afghanistan, except that the hills of Kodekarai were forest-clad while those of his country were bare. But both of them exemplified space and freedom.

Kempekarai is a small hamlet standing on the lower slopes of the western range. Around it lie a few fields and beyond the fields the forest of dense bamboo, intersected by a rocky stream that flows down the centre of the valley.

This valley, which I called 'Spider Valley' because of the immense spiders that spin their webs across the narrow footpath that runs beside the stream, broadens out toward the south into a larger tract known as the Morappur Valley where the rocky stream finally joins the Chinnar river at a spot called Sopathy, some ten miles from the Cauvery river.

I have described the area at some length so that the reader may, with a little imagination, share the stirring beauty: the dank smell of rotting vegetation, the twilight of a dense jungle, the distant half-roar, half-moan of a man-eating tiger searching for its prey, the eerie and deathly silence that follows those thrilling calls, and finally that faint rustle in the undergrowth, the indefinable creeping something that is the man-eater, watching as he becomes aware of your presence

THE MARAUDER OF KEMPEKARAI

and pits the age-long hunting skill of his kind against the civilised intellect of man.

But let me begin my story.

Kempekarai was in a state of great fear, for a man-eating tiger had appeared, and three of its few inhabitants had already gone to fill his bill of fare.

The first victim, an old poojaree, had left Muttur, eleven miles away, to come to Kempekarai one month ago. He was never seen again. Elephants infest these areas, and very occasionally kill men, so when the poojaree failed to arrive at Kempekarai, a search-party set out towards Muttur. Perhaps the men who composed it expected to come upon the plate-like spoor of an elephant, and to find the squashed remains. But they found neither. About five miles from Kempekarai they did come upon the tracks of a male tiger, a little blood by the *path*-side, the old man's staff and his *loincloth*—and, nothing more.

Some ten days later, near sunset, a woman went down to the community well to fill her water-pot for the night. She never returned. At eight p.m. her husband and some of his friends, carrying lanterns and staves, visited the well to look for her. The brass water-pot, half-filled with water, lay on its side some twenty feet from the well, where it had been dropped by the woman on her return to the village. Of her there was no trace.

Next morning, a search-party was instituted, which duly came across the woman's saree, later a silver anklet, and finally her remains. Her head lay under a bush; her hands and feet were scattered about; of the remainder of her body, a goodly number of gnawed bones showed the tiger had indeed been hungry and had done full justice to a succulent repast.

A month dragged by. Kempekarai assumed the air of a fortress besieged. Nobody came in, and nobody went out. The immediate precincts, and in some cases interiors, of the few huts stank with human filth. Was there not a killer nearby, waiting for the first victim who was bold enough to even venture outside to answer the call of nature? The matter was particularly perilous at night; human beings, with their cattle and sometimes their dogs, were barricaded together within their cramped huts behind doors that were kept shut with logs of wood or rounded boulders from the stream. The huts became more filthy every day, under the force of the terrible circumstances in which the people were placed.

But the very best of precautions sometimes fall short of attaining their desired results. Mara, one of the sons-in-law of my old friend Byra, the poojaree, had spurned to live in such insanitary conditions. He had told his wife that, man-eating tiger or not, he for one would not soil the inside of his house. Nightly he had gone outside to answer the calls of nature, and nightly he had returned. Then one night he went out as usual for the same purpose, but this time he did not return. His wife, anxiously waiting inside, admits she heard a dull thud, a rasping gurgle, but nothing more.

After fifteen minutes she raised an alarm. Nobody would come to her rescue, for nobody dared. The inhabitants of the barricaded huts heard her shrieks for help. They knew that by this time Mara was beyond human assistance. He was dead, but they were alive! What was the use of going outside to join him among the dead! So they remained indoors, and listened to her screaming for the remainder of that long night.

Next morning, a half-hearted attempt was made to find what was left of Mara, and it would have been unsuccessful but that the tiger had boldly eaten his fill among the bushes within two hundred yards of the village. A little more was left of Mara than had been left of the woman who had gone to the well. Perhaps his flesh was tougher, or perhaps the tiger was less hungry. Who knows? His head and torso, at least, were still in one piece.

Because of the fate that had befallen his son-in-law, my old friend Byra, who happened to be at Kempekarai at that time, undertook the hazardous eighteen-mile journey to the village of Pennagram next day. He came by himself, as nobody would accompany him, and made the journey without sight or sound of the man-eater. At Pennagram he sought out his old acquaintance, Ranga, and the two of them came by bus to Bangalore. At 9 p.m. that night voices called me to the front door, and, going outside, I was surprised but delighted to see my old jungle companions once more.

The Salem district had meanwhile adopted 'prohibition' as a guiding policy towards physical, moral and, no doubt, spiritual uplift. But my two visitors, being simple, honest forest-folk, with no such high physical, moral or spiritual pretensions, enjoyed a shot of good spirits in the form of half a tumbler of neat brandy, each. Thus refreshed, they began at the beginning, or rather Byra did, and related the brief history of the coming and doings of the man-eater, as I have told it to you, closing with the flat statement that his son-in-law, Mara, must be avenged and that I was to do it.

In the face of that argument and his childlike confidence in me, I could find no very convincing reply. Three days later I was on the road to Pennagram, where I left the Studebaker. We bought supplies at the local market, and within a few hours the three of us were trudging those eighteen miles to the little hamlet of Kemperkarai, where the car could not go.

A couple of miles before our destination we found fresh pug-marks of a tiger on the footpath. No human traveller had passed along this track for many days, and the spoor was clear. I made careful measurements and noted that the pugs belonged to a male tiger of average size. This gave no indication whether the maker was an old animal, or of normal adult age, nor could any of us say at that time whether he was the man-eather, or just another passing tiger.

The few inhabitants of Kempekarai were unable to add much material information to that which had already been given to me by Byra. They thought the man-eater was an enormous animal, but, of course, all simple folk, when keyed up to a state of sheer terror bordering on panic, as had been the case with these poor people for the past few weeks, are given to attributing superhuman cunning and wholly impossible bodily strength and size to their oppressor.

The problem now was: how to proceed, and what to do? The answer was: wait for a kill, or present a live-bait. This particular tiger had not killed a single cow or other domestic animal belonging to the villagers. So far, at least, it had killed only human beings. The question was: would it kill an animal bait, or should that bait be human? To which the only answer was, that in the event of a human bait, it could be nobody but myself, an answer which I thoroughly disliked even to think about.

Byra, Ranga, and myself went into close conference, over successive mugs of tea, and eventually an answer began to take shape. I thought we should try animal baits, but they thought a human bait—myself, of course—would produce immediate results. I heartily wished they had reached a different conclusion.

In a three-man committee, any two of them form an overwhelming majority. The odd man must give in but I managed to force my point to the extent of agreeing that together with the human bait, there would be no harm in trying out a couple of young bullocks at selected spots as an additional attraction.

No buffaloes were available at Kempekarai, so I bought two bullocks, one of which we tied at the spot where we had found the pug-marks, and the other on the bed of the stream that meandered along the bottom of the valley. I sat on the stone parapet of the well, my back resting against one of the wooden uprights that supported the pulley-wheel, through which ran a rope for drawing water. I arranged for a metal pot to be tied to the end of this rope, which I kept beside me on the parapet. Fresh water is always nicer to drink than that from a water-bottle.

The jungle began some fifty yards from the well in all directions except one. Here somebody had planted a dozen or more papaya trees. With the occasional watering from the well that these trees received, an undergrowth, mainly of grass with a few shrubs here and there, had sprung up around the papaya tree. In daylight this undergrowth appeared negligible, but with twilight and approaching darkness, I began to feel it presented an admirable line of approach for the man-eater, which could easily crawl through it on its belly and come within almost springing distance of where I sat, without my being aware of its presence.

When this thought came to my mind, I changed my position to the other side of the well, using the opposite wooden upright as a back-rest, so that I now faced the papayas.

I had only decided to expose myself in view of the fact that we had fortunately come at a time just before full moon. Moonrise almost synchronised with sunset, but I had forgotten that the moon still had to top the range of hills to the east before it could cast its brilliance on that benighted well. This would only happen after 8 p.m. and I spent one of the worst ninety minutes of life awaiting—I cannot hope to express how eagerly and anxiously—the first rays of that longed-for moon.

The experience brought me back to the terrible hours I had spent before the huts of Gummalapur, awaiting that horrid panther, and to the day I had sat with my back to the teak tree, in the far distant Chamala forest range, hoping for a glimpse of a similar man-eater;* and I wondered what had made me so foolish as once again to place myself in such an awkward predicament. Then common sense told me that perhaps it was the only way.

The darkness was deathly still, and not even the familiar nightjar came anywhere near me. A few bats flitted down the well, to sip the limpid water in a series of flying-kisses, as they quenched their thirst after the hot day. I strained my eyes, not only towards the papaya trees, but also in all directions. Imagination created the form of the man-eater, slowly creeping, stealthily stalking me, from just outside my range of vision. I sat glued to the parapet, my .405 cocked, my thumb on the torch-switch.

The thoughts that spring to a man's mind at such times are often strange and unaccountable, but why should I burden you with them? The tiger first assumed the role of possible avenging fate. At other times it practically faded from conscious thought.

Shortly after eight o'clock the skyline above the eastern range grew more distinct; a pale glow diffused itself against the sky, dimming the stars, and then the moon appeared, lightening both the surroundings and my nervous condition. As the moon rose higher in the heavens, the scene became brighter, until I could see almost clearly between the stems of the papaya trees. Not a sound disturbed the silence of my vigil for practically the first half of the night.

Shortly after 11 p.m. a sambar stag voiced its strident call from the bed of the stream where I had tied one of my bullocks. I recognised the note of alarm and fear in its voice, as the call was repeated over and over again, to die away at

---

* See *Nine Man-Eaters and One Rogue*

last in the distance, when the stag ascended the rampart of the opposing range of hills to safety.

Again silence fell, and the night dragged out its last hours. It then struck me that I might perhaps be able to catch the tiger's acute hearing, if he was anywhere within a mile, by operating the pulley-wheel above the well, which, I had noticed earlier in the afternoon, creaked and squealed loudly as it revolved about its uncoiled axle. Perhaps he would hear and be attracted, thinking another prospective victim was drawing water from the well.

So I went around the well to where the water-pot rested on the ground. First of all I stood the firearm up against the wall, and then let the pot down till it touched the water, drawing it up and letting it down in slow succession thereafter. The pulley screeched loudly in the silence of the night, and I continued for nearly an hour, stopping every now and again to survey my surroundings intently, particularly the deep shadows cast by every bush. But nothing stirred, and in the breathless air not a leaf moved, nor did even a belated rat rustle the dried debris that carpeted the ground beneath the adjacent papayas. To all intents and purposes, I was the only living thing in that area, apart from the inmates of the huts, secure behind barricaded doors.

After 3 a.m. the moon began to sink behind the western range of hills, and the same conditions presented themselves as in the previous evening. It grew darker and darker, and soon I could see only a few yards around me, and that by the radiance of the stars that came to life, and twinkled overhead, with the disappearance of the setting moon.

There were only ninety minutes of darkness left, and I felt terribly sleepy. Still I had now to redouble my guard. Had I not been trying to attract the tiger for the past hour? As he had not passed that way all night, it was just possible he might do so now. Moreover, conditions for a surprise attack were all in his favour, as the papaya trees themselves now became undefined, except as a darker blur among the other shadows in my line of vision.

I realised that the man-eater had me completely at his mercy if he chose to attack. Should he roar as he charged, I could at least discharge my rifle at point-blank range. On the other hand, if he crept silently upon me, I would not be aware of his coming until actually struck down.

At the same time, all the rats and rabbits, and other small animals, which had been conspicuous by their absence all night, appeared to select this moment to rendezvous near the well. They scurried hither and thither, and rustled the dead leaves, sometimes noisily, sometimes barely audibly, while my excited imagination telegraphed the urgent message 'the man-eater is coming'.

Altogether I had a dreadful time. The false dawn came and went, and then at 5.45 a.m. the brightening of the skyline once more, above the eastern range, told me that daylight was at last at hand and that the tedious vigil was nearly over. It was well past seven before the sun peeped over the eastern hills, and I arose and dragged my wary, sleepy steps to the tent I had pitched at the southern end of the village.

Hot tea and a nap till ten-thirty. Then, accompanied by Ranga and Byra, I first visited the bait tethered in the streambed. It was alive and well. Closer inspection showed that a tiger had approached to within 15 feet of it and had passed on after a cursory inspection.

The sambar stag I had heard during the night had doubtless seen or scented this tiger and had voiced his loud alarm. The tiger's pug-marks were clearly identified as having been made by the same animal as had been those I had seen while coming along the *path* on the western range, where the ground was firmer and dimensions not exaggerated. Nevertheless, I had little doubt that this was the real maneater, for a normal tiger will not readily leave a tempting, unguarded bait alive.

We then went to see the other bullock, where a surprise awaited us. It had been killed by a tiger, whose pug-marks were identical with those I had carefully measured the previous day, near the very same spot on the pathway.

The question now was this: were there two tigers in the vicinity, or had the second bullock been killed by the man-eater? If the latter was the case and there was only one tiger—and that the man-eater—why had he not killed the bullock which had been tied in the streambed instead of just looking at it and choosing to kill the other?

I formed the definite opinion that there were two tigers in the vicinity, and that it had been the man-eater which had ignored the bullock at the stream. Ranga agreed with me, but Byra would not commit himself to either opinion. He suggested that the man-eater might be the only tiger in the area, that it had not killed the first bullock, possibly because it was a white one. The second, being dark brown, had been above suspicion.

On the question of the colour of a live-bait I have a very open mind. In my own experience, colour makes little or no difference to a tiger, and he will kill your bait provided certain other conditions also exist. He must be hungry, for a tiger rarely, if ever, kills wantonly. Moreover, he must not suspect a trap of any kind. In these days when tiger-hunting is becoming intensified, tigers are learning their lessons quickly. Nature makes an effort to try to preserve a species which is rapidly becoming shot-out.

Thus a bait secured around the neck by a rope stands a very good chance of not being touched by a tiger. He cannot reason, but his instinct, or sense of self-preservation, tells him that it is unnatural of villagers to tie up their cattle for the night in a forest. A bait secured by a rope tied around the horns stands more chance of being killed, for it is possible for an animal to get entangled in the under-growth by its horns. A bait secured by its hind leg is also readily taken. The main point to be remembered is that both tigers and panthers attack the throats of their victims, and there should therefore be no visible obstruction to prevent this method of attack, or the attacker becomes suspicious.

Panthers are generally less careful than tigers in this respect, and take greater risks. Personally, I dislike tethering dogs as bait for a panther; I feel the practice is extremely cruel, for the dog is a very sagacious animal and knows well the purpose for which he is being tied. This being so, he must suffer terrible mental torture till his attacker arrives. When I was younger, and, I must confess, had fewer scruples, I tried to salve my conscience by protecting the dog's life. To achieve this I made a collar about four inches broad, using two pieces of leather, with numerous two-inch-long, sharpened nails in close array, protruding outwards, the heads of the nails coming between the two strips of leather. It would amuse me, in those bygone days, to watch the panther grab at the dog's throat, only to spring backwards in obvious dismay as the sharp nails pierced his mouth. Before he could solve the puzzle, of course, he was shot. But such elementary tricks cannot be played on a tiger.

Tying up a sickly live-bait is also fatal to success. The Badaga tribe, who inhabit the Nilgiri mountains, are very averse to selling healthy animals for bait, no matter what price is offered for them. They feel it is a sin to sacrifice the life of a good bullock. Invariably, they will offer only a sickly animal, whose days are numbered anyhow, for this purpose.

THE MARAUDER OF KEMPEKARAI

I well remember tying up a bullock in the last stages of foot-and-mouth disease. For three nights in succession, as tracks in the sand revealed, the tiger came to the spot, walked around the bait, even squatted before it, and then decided it was too diseased to kill. On the fourth night, my son sat up over the sick animal, but by eight o'clock its allotted span of life was running out. It collapsed and took the whole night to die. That night the tiger did not even appear.

Hunters of experience vary in their opinions regarding the colour of a live-bait, and I have met a few who avoid using white animals, either cattle or goats, because they claim that these are the least likely to be taken. A famous panther-hunter of days gone by, who had shot over a hundred panthers, was very averse to tying up a black goat, which, he claimed, made the panther extra wary in its approach.

I have digressed at some length on these points, as I feel many of you who read these stories will be interested to learn what might be called some aspects of the technique of tiger and panther shooting. In drawing-room circles we often hear of the extraordinary degree of 'good luck' that attends a certain *shikari* or big-game hunter. Actually, much of this 'good luck' is due to his previous experience of the innumerable factors that combine to make, or mar, a successful hunt.

Returning, to my story. There was obviously only one thing to do, and that was to fix a *machan* above the partly eaten brown bullock. Through experience both our baits had been tethered near suitable trees; so while I went back to the tent for a further nap, Ranga and Byra, both highly qualified in such matters, made a good job of slinging up the canvas camp-chair I had brought, neatly folded, with me. Next to a *charpoy*, or Indian rope-cot, a folding chair makes a good *machan*. It is not nearly so comfortable or roomy as the *charpoy*, but has an advantage in being easily taken to pieces and folded up.

Returning by 5 p.m., I took up my position, prepared for an all-night vigil.

The pathway, situated as it was on the western range above the village of Kempekarai, received the rays of the rising moon far earlier than did the village and the well, where I had spent the previous night. So it was that, soon after the sun sank below the western hill-tops, the moon peeped over the eastern range, and visibility was good all around me.

Nothing happened till shortly after eight, when I became aware that the tiger stood directly beneath me. How or from where it had come, I never knew. Certainly not along the *path* which was clearly visible in both directions as it stretched away into the forest. I knew the tiger was below me by the soft noise it made as it rubbed its body against the trunk of the tree in which I was sitting, and in doing so looked up and became aware of my presence!

Things then began to happen quickly. With a snarling growl, the tiger began at once to claw its way up the tree trunk. Fortunately, we had selected a tree with fairly straight trunk till the first crotch was reached at about fifteen feet above the ground—where I was sitting on the camp chair. I knew that this was the man-eater, for normally a tiger would have decamped at once on becoming aware that a human being sat above him.

Instinctively I drew up both legs as high as possible, while leaning over the chair sideways and to the left, to get in a shot. Unfortunately, I had leant in the wrong direction, for the tiger was trying to climb the tree on my right side. I quickly corrected myself, but now had to hold the rifle to my left shoulder.

It took you longer to read the preceding two paragraphs than events actually took that night. As I have said, I was sitting about fifteen feet above the ground. A normal tiger is about nine feet long from nose-tip to tail-tip. Subtracting the length of his tail and adding something in compensation for an outstretched forepaw, we may come by a working figure of almost 8 feet to cover the 'stretching range' of man-eater, or for that matter, of any tiger. Deducting these eight feet from the original height of fifteen feet, we get a difference of about seven feet, which was about the distance that the tiger succeeded in climbing the tree-trunk that night. In his eagerness to get hold of me he stretched out a forepaw, and as the sharp claws drove through the canvas of the camp-chair seat, and incidentally partially through my pants, the tiger lost his balance and fell backwards to earth, while instinctively, in my anxiety to protect my rear, I half-levered myself out of the chair. I was lucky not to drop my rifle and follow in the wake of the tiger.

Now it is a peculiar fact about man-eaters, both tigers and panthers, that they appear to be craven creatures, although they attack and devour human beings. Almost without exception, such attacks are made from behind, and when the victim is not aware of the presence of his attacker. Very rarely, indeed, has any man-eater been known to carry out frontal attack or rush a person who is aware of his presence and faces him.

So it was that night, for, as he fell backwards to earth, the man-eater realised his presence had been disclosed, and no sooner had he landed on the ground than, with a bound and a snarl, he disappeared in the surrounding lantana.

I cannot say to which of our good fortunes it was that he did so, for, although I had now become aware of his presence and was prepared for him, I might easily have overbalanced, or dropped the rifle, in trying to get a downward shot at that very awkward angle, directly below me. Be that as it may, he was gone in a flash, and as suddenly and as unexpectedly as he had come.

My presence having been discovered, there was now no point in remaining motionless or silent. Reviewing the damage done, I discovered three claw-marks through the canvas of the chair, each about five inches long, where the tiger's forepaw had swept. Of these, two had penetrated the seat of my pants — and myself inside them to a lesser extent. The flesh certainly smarted, to remind me of the fact.

Normally, the incident would evoke some mirth in the minds of mirthful people, but I would remind them that the claws of all carnivores are full of poisonous bacteria from the decomposed flesh at which they tear, and a man-eater is no exception to this rule, because the flesh happens to be human. The canvas of the chair, and the cloth of my pants, were not sufficiently thick to absorb all this poisonous material, so that there was some chance of my wound becoming infected.

I had brought with me a variety of first aids, including a good stock of procaine penicillin and my five c.c. hypodermic syringe. But all these were in my tent at Kempekarai, some two miles away. I had therefore to choose between returning immediately and taking medical precautions, or remaining till morning—which was at least ten hours ahead—by which time the poison might have spread in the wounds. In the one case I had to face the chance of an attack by the man-eater, which might be launched anywhere along the *path* for the distance of the two miles it extended up to Kempekarai. On the other hand, I had to face perhaps the more certain danger of sepsis, and a long period of incapacitation from pursuing the man-eater.

So I chose to risk the tiger, as the lesser of the two evils, and quickly letting my rifle down on the rope brought for the purpose, I quickly scrambled down myself, praying fervently that the man-eater would not choose that very moment for a second attack. Reaching the ground, I stood with my back to the tree-trunk, while I freed the rifle from the rope by which I had lowered it. All was as silent as the grave, and not a sound came from any part of the forest to give me any indication of the whereabouts of my recent attacker. For all intents and purposes he might be ten miles away, or behind the nearest bush! The brilliant moonlight bathed the jungle in its ethereal glow, making visible each leaf and grass-blade as they gracefully vibrated to the soft currents of the night-breezes that gently wafted the scent of night flowers along the glades of the forest, or blew in gusts between the aisles of its myriad trees.

After a few moments, I set forth along the *path* on the two-mile walk to Kempekarai. Now this *path* varies in width according to the nature of the soil, and the character of the vegetation, from fifteen feet at the maximum to hardly a yard. At certain spots it is fringed with long grass and at other places by lantana undergrowth. Several small streams have to be crossed, where bamboos grow in profusion, their tall swaying stems creaking to the gentle breeze, while the fronds, in obliterating the moonlight, cast ghostly, chequered patterns on the ground in front.

In such circumstances your heart thumps in your chest almost audibly and as if to leap from its cage; your nerves are frayed to breaking-point and every faint rustle heralds the man-eater's charge. The inclination is to hurry, if not break into a run. Your nerves signal you to look to one side or the other, for the tiger may be making an attack from behind or from either side!

All these emotions must be held under close restraint, for to give way to them in the least would mean panic, and panic will cause you to lose your presence of mind, with ultimate but certain destruction to follow.

The thing to make certain of is that the tiger is not in front, lying in ambush till you come abreast of him. To attack from the rear, he has to make at least some noise in the undergrowth in order to catch up with your normal stride as you walk forward.

It is wisest, therefore, to look in front, although your eyes must search every shadow before you come abreast of it, rather than keep turning the head from side to side. Keep your rifle cocked and held in the crook of your arm, for you will have to fire from your hip, and make certain of your shot. There will be no time to raise the rifle to your shoulder and aim, for the tiger is a killer, and it is not the habit of killers, either animal or human, to go about advertising their presence. For if they did, they would soon cease to be the killer—and become the 'killed' instead.

If your quarry is wounded, you may perhaps hear a snarl or growl, but most likely that unnervingly awful, earth-shaking *'woof'* as he charges. If he is not wounded, and a man-eater, you may expect to hear just nothing, for he will be upon you in the twinkling of an eye.

Hardly a quarter-of-a-mile before Kempekarai there is a low outcrop of boulders on both sides of the *path*. This is the most dangerous spot in the journey home, as the tiger could be behind any one of those boulders. However, seeing him head the other way when he made off, I felt he had not had enough time to retrace his steps. With this mental assurance, I negotiated the rocks, and soon came to Kempekarai and my tent.

Ranga and Byra were awake, as they always remained when I went out alone, in case I should require their sudden assistance. Telling them to make a fire and heat some water, I drank some coffee that had been kept ready, and got out my hypodermic, which I sterilized in the hot water. Thereafter, mixing two phials of eight-lakh units of procaine penicillin, I gave myself a shot with the syringe.

THE MARAUDER OF KEMPEKARAI

I got Ranga and Byra to wash the wounds with a strong solution of potassium permanganate dissolved in the rest of the hot water, followed by a dressing of sulphonomide ointment. The spot was one that could not be bandaged, or plastered, so I went to sleep hoping that no ill effects would develop with my wounds.

I was tired after my sleepless nights, and it was nearly nine before I awoke next morning. This is a very late hour for rising in any jungle, where one is usually up and out before sunrise. The wounds, I was glad to note, were not unduly painful.

Taking another four lakhs of penicillin, and after redressing the wounds, I breakfasted excellently on porridge, bacon and eggs, and an enormously large, ripe papaya fruit from the grove by the well-side, where I had spent the first night.

Then I set off to visit my bait on the streambed, which I found as alive and well as on the previous morning. Returning the two miles up the *path* to where I had sat the previous night, I found the tiger had not come back nor touched the bullock he had killed two nights before. His pug-marks, as he had approached the tree, identified him as the tiger whose prints I had seen first.

The forests of Salem, unlike those of the Nilgiris, Coimbatore and Chittoor districts, are mostly thorny in nature, lantana and the 'wait-a-bit' thorn predominating. Along the valleys and streambeds these give way to clumps of bamboo, massed in close array. In either case, the effect is the same, namely, to make roaming or stalking unprofitable, if not impossible.

A carnivore moves silently, and the secret of its success as a hunter lies in the animal instinctively watching where it places its front paw in order to make no sound. Next it places its rear paw in exactly the same spot, as the front paw moves forward again to take the next step. The human stalker must move silently, too. He must watch carefully where he places each step, for the smallest dry leaf will crackle when trodden upon; the smallest twig will snap. Those clutching 'wait-a-bit' thorns must be avoided, too, for a single thorn is strong enough to halt your progress if it catches in any part of your clothing, while it will rip your flesh in no uncertain manner if you are foolish enough to wear shorts.

All this will distract your attention from being on the lookout for the tiger, and if that tiger is a man-eater, who will not be deterred by thorns, you are at a distinct disadvantage.

The jungle at this spot was etremely thorny, so we returned to Kempekarai to hold a council of war with the 'greybeards' of the village. The facts, as far as we now knew them, showed that:

The man-eater was a male of average size.

He particularly frequented the *path* on the western range.

He did not particularly care for bullock meat.

We were still uncertain whether or not there was a second tiger in the vicinity.

The obvious conclusion reached after this discussion was much the same as that reached by Ranga, Byra and myself on the first day we had come to Kempekarai: either await the next human kill, or offer a human live-bait, preferably somewhere along the pathway to Kempekarai as it descends the western ridge. A couple of bullocks could also be tied out elsewhere in the jungle to tempt the man-eater, but more to find out if there was another tiger operating in the same area.

The scratches which the tiger had inflicted, being located where they were, made it impossible for me to sit still for more than fifteen minutes at a stretch. This fact precluded all chances of 'sitting-up', in the literal meaning of the word. True, if I was to act as a bait there would be no necessity for me to sit still. In fact, movement would be a necessary factor in helping to attract the tiger. On the other hand, the very act of sitting would not only be agonising, but would also retard the healing of the wounds, which I was naturally anxious to hasten.

The alternatives left were either to stand or lie down. The former course was naturally not advisable for a night-long vigil, so the only practical method under the circumstances was to lie down.

We did a lot of thinking that day and eventually came by what we all thought to be a very ingenious plan. How ingenious it actually turned out—or rather did not turn out to be—you will very soon come to know.

I have already explained that the footpath down the western range to Kempekarai was crossed at several places by streamlets, bordered by dense undergrowth and clumps of bamboo. The beds of these small rivulets were rocky and admirably suited the purpose I had in mind.

It so happened that the first of these small streams to be crossed on the way down to Kempekarai, from the tree on which I had sat the night before, was the broadest of the lot, and was, moreover, closely covered with rounded boulders of all sizes. My plan was to detach a cart-wheel from one of the only two bullock-carts in the village of Kempekarai, dig a pit in the stream-bed, get inside it, place the wheel above, and anchor it securely around the circumference with big boulders. Smaller boulders, and a camouflage of dry leaves, would help to conceal the cartwheel. I would also make a human dummy and seat it somewhere on the footpath, where it crossed the stream. The cartwheel would be raised off the ground at one end, facing the dummy, to allow me a range of fire in that direction.

This was my general plan. For the benefit of those who have not been to India, I would explain that the wheel of an Indian bullock-cart—I am referring to the large type of cart—averages five feet in diameter. The circumference is of wood, some six inches wide by three inches thick, shod with a hoop of iron to serve as a tyre. There are a dozen stout wooden spokes, all converging on a massive central wooden hub. The central hole in the wooden hub rotates around an iron axle, some one-and-a-half inches thick. The wheel is kept from falling off by a cotter-pin in the form of a flat iron nail, passing through the axle at its outer extremity. Similarly, the wheel is prevented from moving towards the frame of the cart by the axle itself, which is made suddenly thicker immediately beyond the bearing surface of the axle on the hub, which is perhaps a little over a foot in width. In what may be called deluxe models, a better bearing surface is provided by lining the hole in the wooden hub with a piece of iron or galvanised piping. 'High-grade lubrication', from the village viewpoint, is provided by applying old motor oil, perhaps once a fortnight, on the ends of the axle, after removing the cotter-pin and the wheel to do so. The oil is carried permanently on the cart in the shell of an old bullock-horn, suspended somewhere beneath the cart, and is applied to the axle at the end of any piece of stick that may happen to be lying handy, when 'servicing time' comes up.

It was too late to set the cartwheel that day, so we busied ourselves gathering old clothing from the villagers. Pants are unknown in such parts, so I contributed a pair of mine, into which we stuffed two 'legs', made of bamboo and wound around with straw. In case the pants might strike the tiger as being unfamiliar, we draped a *'dhoti'* (which is a cross between a sarong and a *loincloth*) over the pants. The body of the dummy consisted of straw rammed into an old gunny sack, over which we draped a couple of torn shirts, and a very ragged coat. The head of the dummy was a work of art; it was made from a large-sized coconut, complete with its coir fibre.

On dress occasions Indian women sometimes augment their natural hair with 'false hair', which they twist into a 'bun' or 'coonday' behind their heads, into which they stick flowers, particularly jasmine. Fortunately there was a 'belle' in Kemperkarai who was vain enough to be the owner of a coil of such hair. This we borrowed, combed out, and fixed around the coconut, to emulate the long hair of a villager. An untidily-tied, 'yokel-pattern' turban was then wound around the nut and a pair of 'chappals' or sandals were put on the dummy's feet.

Tigers, as I have said, have no sense of smell, so the dummy looked realistic enough to attract a man-eater, if only he did not watch it long enough to begin wondering at its uncanny stillness.

That night I applied fresh dressing to my wounds, and next morning helped myself to another shot of penicillin. I was thankful to note that so far no undue inflammation had occurred.

By 8 a.m. half-a dozen willing helpers and myself had trundled the cartwheel to the crossing I had in mind. Here we busied ourselves excavating a hole nearly four feet across by about four feet deep. This was easily done, for we were digging in the soft sand of a streambed. Some grass was then cut and thrown into the hole to absorb, to some degree, the dampness of the sand which naturally increased with the digging of the hole.

Sitting inside, I found I could adopt only a semi-crouched position, which was going to be very uncomfortable indeed, the only recommendation it offered being that it saved me from a sitting position, which, as I have said already, would have been most uncomfortable in view of my recent wounds.

The dummy we placed with its back to a tamarind tree, some fifteen feet away, which stood on the western bank of the stream where it was crossed by the track to Kempekarai; it was so arranged that its legs stuck out on the track at an angle of forty-five degrees. Thus, it would at once be visible to the tiger from any point along the streambed or on either section of the track, if he happened to pass in any of those directions. Lastly, we collected some of the larger boulders, and, as I stood guard with my rifle, Ranga and Byra gathered brushwood and debris for camouflaging the wheel.

When eventually I got into the hole, the wheel was just a couple of inches above the top of my head. There was a space of six inches between the ground level and the wheel through which I could fire in the direction of the dummy; it was made by placing two stones of that size about three feet apart under the circumference, leaving the central portion open to the sky for the purpose of ventilation. Brushwood and debris were scattered and intertwined among the boulders; it would also give me warning if he came up from behind, when the debris would crackle as he brushed against it or trod on it.

For safety's sake, I had arranged that the men should return to Kempekarai in a body, and only come back next morning, again in a body. I would be imprisoned all night in the hole, as the weight of the cartwheel with the boulders above it was too great for me to lift unaided from inside.

It was 4.30 p.m. when I entered my voluntary prison. It had taken nearly another half-hour to position the boulders on the wheel and arrange the camouflage, so that it was almost five when I found myself alone. The heat inside the hole, despite the opening above, was stifling. I removed my coat and shirt, and would have removed the remainder of my clothes but for the fact that I did not want the sand to get into my wounds.

Peeping above the level of the ground, I could clearly distinguish the dummy and quite a wide extent of the background. A clump of 'henna' bushes grew halfway down the sloping bank behind the dummy. A slight movement in that direction caught my eye, which I found was due to the twitching, outstretched ear of a beautiful spotted stag that gazed in curiosity at the motionless dummy. The value of sitting still in a forest was then made apparent to me, for the stag gazed a full ten minutes at that still dummy. Then it appeared to lose interest in the curious object, came out on to the open track, which it eventually crossed, vanishing into the jungle on the other side. The distance between the dummy and the stag could not have been much more than twenty feet, and yet the latter was quite unalarmed. Had a human been seated in place of the dummy, he would surely have moved, even if it was an eyelid that flickered, and this would have sent the stag crashing away in alarm.

A pair of peafowl then came strutting along the track. The cock-bird stopped, fanned out his tail and rustled the quills in display to his admiring spouse. Female-like, she kept one eye on him and the other elsewhere! Anyway, she saw the dummy, took a short run, and sailed into the air. The cock, chagrined at her failure to appreciate his beauty, lowered his tail and saw the dummy too. A much heavier bird than the hen, he flapped wildly and desperately in an effort to take off, his wings beating loudly on the still evening air, before he finally managed to rise just clear of the surrounding bushes and follow his more wary partner to apparent safety.

'Kuck-kaya-kaya-khuck' crowed the grey junglecocks in all directions, as they came out along the streambed to peck a few morsels before darkness fell. 'Kukurruka-wack-kukurruka-wack' cackled the smaller spurfowl, belligerent little birds, as male fought male in little duels throughout the jungle for the favour of an accompanying hen. Drab and uninteresting as she looks, to gain her favour was for them the only interest in the world that evening.

Darkness fell, to the farewell call of the pair of peafowl, as they roosted for the night on some tall tree in the forest, perhaps a quarter-of-a-mile away. 'Mia-a-oo-Aaow' they cried, as the sun sank behind the western range.

Those of you who have been in an Indian forest will remember the almost miraculous switch-over that takes place at sunset, as the birds of the daylight hours cease their calls, and the birds of the night take up theirs. 'Chuck-chuk-chuk-chucko' cried the nightjars, as with widespread wings they sailed overhead in search of insect morsels, or settled on the ground, resembling stones against a background of sand.

It was pitch-dark where I sat and even the dummy was hidden under the shadows of the tamarind tree beneath which it was propped. I reckoned the moonlight would not reach that spot till after ten. At nine I heard the noisy snuffling and deep-throated gurgle of a sloth bear, as it wended its clumsy way down the stream in my direction. It almost fell over the outlying debris we had placed on the streambed to give me warning of the tiger's approach, and then saw the newly-heaped boulders placed upon the cartwheel! I could have read the thoughts that crossed the little brain beneath the shaggy black hair! 'Here's a chance to find some luscious fat grubs, or a beetle or two; perhaps a nest of white ants, or, most hopeful of all, a beehive built by the small yellow bees that can hardly sting a big bear like me.'

With those thoughts, the bear fell to work on the task of clearing away the boulders that so carefully anchored my cartwheel.

'Shoo!' I whispered in an undertone. 'Get away, you interfering...!'

THE MARAUDER OF KEMPEKARAI

The bear heard my voice, and stopped. 'Where did that come from?' he was thinking. A few minutes' silence followed, and then he started at the stones again. 'Out! Shoo!' I whispered. The bear stopped, climbed over the boulders, and looked down between the spokes at me.

'Aa-rr, Wr-rrr!' he growled. 'Get out, you idiot!' I growled. 'Wr-oof! Wr-oof! Wr-oof' he answered, as he scrambled, helter-skelter, over the boulders, stumbled over the debris, scampered up the bank and crashed away between the dried bamboos.

Hardly ten minutes had passed after the bear's noisy departure when I heard the most infinitesimal of noises, the soft tread of the padded foot of some heavy animal. It is almost impossible to imitate that noise in speech, and less so on paper. The nearest description I can give is the very muffled impact of a soft cushion when it is thrown on to a sofa.

The tiger had come and in his silent way was negotiating the fringe of the debris we had scattered on the streambed behind me. He was picking his way carefully across it.

Would he attack the dummy? Would he pass in front of me? These were the questions that raced through my mind as I awaited developments. My nerves were taut with anticipation.

The moon had already risen, but its beams had not yet reached the shadows cast by the heavy foliage of the tamarind tree. The dummy was not visible to me, but I knew that the tiger could clearly see it.

There was silence for a time—how long I could not say. Then came the clink of a stone as it rolled above my head. Nobody had anticipated an attack in that direction; but my recent visitor, the bear, had already shown that the unexpected could happen. Now the unexpected was being repeated by the presence of the tiger above me. What had caused it to ignore the dummy, and come straight to the spot where I lay, was a mystery. Very likely, the tiger had been watching the bear, had seen its strange behaviour, had noted its hurried departure and had come to investigate. Even more likely, the behaviour of the bear had caused the tiger to suspect human agency, which he had come over to find out himself. Or perhaps the wheel just happened to be situated on the shortest line of approach which the tiger was following to get at the dummy.

Whatever be the reason, the tiger was now barely two yards away, and above me.

As these thoughts raced through my mind, I heard the vague sound caused by the tiger's breathing. Then he stepped gracefully over one of the big boulders that held down the wheel, and peered down at me.

In the meantime I had not been idle. Screwing myself around, as best as I could, I now lay half on my back, gazing up at the tiger. The rifle I had drawn inwards and backwards till the butt came up against the side of the hole. I have already told you this hole was about four feet across, and about the same in depth. Hence it was impossible to get the rifle to point completely upwards. The most I could manage was an angle of a little more then sixty degrees with the bottom of the hole. Unfortunately, the tiger was not in the direction in which the muzzle was pointing, but was standing behind it, and directly above the spot where the butt of my rifle was stuck against the side of the hole.

Then events moved quickly. The tiger did not react quite as the bear had done. His features, dimly visible above me, contorted into a hideous snarl. A succession of deep-throated growls issued from his cavernous chest, and, lying down upon the cartwheel, he attempted to rake me with the claws of a foreleg, which he inserted between the spokes of the wheel.

I knew those talons would rip my face and head to ribbons if they only made contact, so, sinking as low into the hole as possible, I struggled desperately to turn the muzzle of the rifle towards the tiger.

All this took only seconds to happen. The tiger growled and came a little farther on to the wheel. The muzzle of my rifle contacted his shoulder and I pressed the trigger.

The explosion, within that confined space, was deafening. The tiger roared hideously as he catapulted backwards. During the next thirty seconds he bit the boulders, the wheel and even the sand, as he gave forth roar after roar of agony. Then I heard him fall amidst the debris, pick himself up, fall again, get up and finally crash into the bushes that bordered the little stream. He was still roaring, and continued to do so for quite fifteen minutes more as he staggered away into the jungle.

Finally silence, total and abysmal, fell over the forest. After the pandemonium that had just reigned, every creature, including the insects, decided it was wise to hide till with the passage of time they could forget their fright.

The hours passed. At one in the morning a stiff breeze began to blow over the hills, dark storm-clouds scudded across the sky, completely hiding the moon, and soon the distant sound of falling rain across the western range fell upon my listening ears. Not long afterwards, large raindrops penetrated between the spokes and splashed down upon me.

Then the deluge began, such as can only be experienced in tropical countries, and particularly forest regions with dense vegetation. I was soaked to the skin, and the water began to trickle down the sides of the hole. With that came the sudden realisation that the stream, which had been dry, would soon be flowing with the spate of rain-water that was running into it from all directions along a hundred tributaries. I would be drowned like a rat in a hole.

Jerked into frenzied action, I got on my hands and knees, placed my back to the wheel and pressed upwards with all my might. The wheel did not budge an inch! My helpers had done their work of protecting me from the tiger only too well! They had placed the heaviest boulders they could find around the circumference of the wheel and I was unable to move them unaided.

There was but one chance left, and that was to dig myself out through the six-inch-wide gap we had made for me to fire through. Desperately, with both hands I scooped the earth downwards into the hole, which was already half filled with water and sand; the damp sides were collapsing, making it very obvious that within the next few minutes, unless I got out quickly, cartwheel and boulders would all come down together on top of me.

When I judged there was sufficient room for my body to pass, I pushed the rifle between the spokes of the wheel and then rested it across them. Next I started squeezing myself through the opening I had just dug, wriggling in the sand and water like a stranded eel, till I finally struggled free onto the streambed.

The rain continued to fall in torrents. I had no idea how far the tiger had gone, or in which direction, so, picking up the rifle, I first carried the dummy off the streambed and placed it high up on the western bank. Then I started to recross the stream on the return journey to Kempekarai, and as I did so, I heard the dull roar of the spate of rain-water descending the streambed from the direction of the hills.

Within a few minutes it arrived, a wall of foaming water over three feet high, carrying all before it. Logs of wood, uprooted trees, dead bamboos and flotsam and jetsam of every description mingled with the crested, frothing waters. They reached the cartwheel and covered it; then the cart-

THE MARAUDER OF KEMPEKARAI

wheel and boulders were swept away downstream along with the torrent. In less than five minutes the stream had become a raging river, over four feet deep.

Thankfully appreciating the escape I had had, I began the return journey to Kempekarai. No other sound could possibly be heard above the splatter and swish of the rain. The darkness was intense, my torch throwing a circle of light before me. Moreover, the ground was extremely slippery to the soft rubber shoes that I was wearing. I had to cross three other streams, slightly smaller that the one where I sat, but all were raging torrents of water.

Half-way to Kempekarai, I saw the flicker of an approaching light. A little later, I met the party of men that were carrying it—Ranga, Byra and a few stalwarts from the village. They had realised the danger I was in when the waters rose and had risked encounter with the man-eater to come to my rescue.

Next morning the sun shone brightly on the saturated forest. We returned to the site of my adventure the night before. All streams were flowing briskly, although they were now no more than two feet deep. There was no trace of the cartwheel anywhere near the crossing. Evidently it had been borne downstream by the spate and probably smashed to bits. We combed both banks thereafter, without finding any signs of the tiger. The torrential rain had only too effectively obliterated any blood-trail or pug-marks.

Two hours later, a depressed and disappointed group, we returned to Kempekarai. There I remained for three more days, hoping to hear news of the tiger, only to be doomed to disappointment. Both Byra and Ranga felt it had died of its wounds, but I doubted this very much, as I knew I had not been able to aim sufficiently well to score more than a mere raking shot.

My period of leave, taken for the purpose of shooting this animal, had now elapsed, so I left Kempekarai on the morning of the fourth day, instructing Ranga to remain behind to assist Byra in reconnoitring. They were then to come to Pennagram, and thence to Dharmapuri, where there was a telegraph office from which they could send me a message. They were to await my reply there.

Ten days after returning to Bangalore, the hoped-for telegram arrived, stating that a pack-pony belonging to a Forest Guard of the Kodekarai Forest Lodge had been killed. Calculating from the telegram that the kill would be four days old by the time I reached it, I sent a reply, telling my henchmen to return to Kempekarai and wait there for any further events, which were to be reported by telegram in the same way.

Six more days passed, when I received a second telegram stating that a tiger had attacked the driver of a bullock-cart that was the last of a convoy travelling from the small hamlet of Morappur towards Sopathy on the Chinar River.

This, no doubt, was the man-eater again. Within an hour I was on my way by car to Dharmapuri, where I picked up my two henchmen. We continued to Pennagram, where we left the car and made a cross-country trip of about twelve miles to Morappur, passing the Chinar river and Sopathy on the way.

I had meanwhile learned that the cartman, who had been attacked by the tiger, had saved his life by jumping from the cart, in which he was travelling, on to the yoke and then between the two bulls that were hauling his cart. He had yelled vociferously and his yells were taken up by the other cartmen in the 'convoy'. The tiger had then made off.

I spoke to this cartman at Morappur. He said that the tiger had suddenly appeared behind his cart, which was the last in the line, and had attempted to leap into it from the rear, when he had dived between his bulls for protection. Asking him why the tiger had not succeeded in the comparatively easy task of getting into the cart, the man said it had jumped half-in, and he had not waited to see any more.

Meanwhile, a party of travellers who had followed us from Sopathy brought the news that they had come across fresh tiger pug-marks, made the previous night, leading down the Chinar River.

Hearing this, we hurried back to Sopathy, and it did not take us long to find the pug-marks. The water was running in the Chinar as a silvery stream, meandering from bank to bank, and in the soft, wet sand we clearly noticed that the tiger which had made the marks must have been limping badly. The weight of the body fell almost entirely on the left forefoot, the right being placed very lightly on the sand at each step.

I have said that, 'Spider Valley' met the Chinar river at this spot. A half-mile downstream, and in the direction in which the tiger had gone, was a small longish rock in midstream. It rose some four feet above the bed of the river and was about forty feet long by eight feet wide. I decided to sit on top of that rock that night, in the hope the tiger might make his way back up the Chinar and see me in my elevated position.

Borrowing Ranga's turban, old brown coat and *dhoti*, I donned all three, the two latter above my own clothing, and seated myself on the rock by 5.30 p.m. As Ranga and Byra were afraid to return to Morappur alone, they elected to spend the night on comfortable crotches, high up in the huge *muthee* trees that border the Chinar in this locality.

The nights were dark at this time, but from my position on the rock, and as the Chinar was about 100 yards wide at this spot, I relied upon the white sand to reflect the starlight and to reveal the form of the tiger from whatever direction it might come. Apart from being handicapped by its lameness, I knew the tiger would not charge its prey from a distance of fifty yards, but would try to stalk as close to me as possible before launching the final attack.

After testing my lighting equipment, I carefully loaded and cocked the .405, which I laid on the rock to my right, where it could not be seen by the tiger and create suspicion. I had also taken the precaution of bringing my .12 bore double-barrel Jeffries with me as a spare weapon. With L.G. slugs in the choke barrel, and lethal-ball in the right, I laid the Jeffries on the rock to my left. My flask of tea, some *chappaties* to satisfy my hunger towards morning, and my pipe completed my creature wants for the night. I sat on my great-coat, for the cushion it provided against that hard rock; I would wear it if the night should become too cold.

The usual animal and bird calls from the forest bade farewell to the day, while the denizens of the night welcomed their turn of activity with their less melodious, and more eerie, cries.

At seven-thirty it was dark; the reflecting whiteness of the sands of the Chinar surrounded my rock as if it were an island.

Just after nine there was a loud bustling and crashing and a tusker came down the bank, walked along the sands, passed the rock where I sat motionless, and continued beyond. There he met the current of breeze blowing down the river and caught scent of me. Banging the end of his trunk against the ground, and emitting a peculiar sound as if a sheet of zinc were being rapidly bent in half, he turned around, smelled more of me and hurried up the bank into the cover of the thick undergrowth that grew there. Such is the behaviour of an elephant when it is not a rogue.

At eleven I was still keeping my watch in all directions, as I had been doing since sunset. Then, half to the rear and my left, I sensed rather than saw a movement. Looking more intently, I could see nothing. No, wait! Was that not a blur against the faint greyish-white carpet of river sand? I looked away and then back again at the spot where I had just noticed the blur. It was not there!

'That's funny', I thought. 'Are my eyes playing tricks, or are they just becoming tired?'

Staring hard, I saw it again. Only it was much closer to me this time than when I had seen it first. Indeed, it was halfway between the further bank and the rock on which I sat.

I could not now risk looking in any other direction until I succeeded in defining this strange object. And as I looked it seemed to stretch, to float towards me, growing longer and shorter at intervals, but making no sound whatever.

Then in a flash I realized what it was. The tiger was crawling towards me on his belly, silently, in quick, short motions, till he judged he was within range to make his final, murderous assault.

Perspiration poured down my face and neck; I trembled with terror and excitement. But this would not do; so taking a deep breath and holding it, to allay the trembling, I offered a silent prayer to my Maker and drew the rifle on to my lap, raising it to my shoulder.

The tiger, now some twenty yards away, saw my movement and seemed to guess that his presence had been discovered. A thin black streak, his tail moved behind him. The blur became compact as he gathered himself for the charge. My torch-beam fell full on his snarling, flattened head. Then the rifle spoke, a split-second before he sprang.

With my bullet he rose and bounded forward. I owe my life to the fact that the torch did not go out, and I was able to fire a second shot. Then he had reached the rock.

Because of his earlier wound, or my recent shots—at that moment I could not tell which—he failed to climb up. My third bullet, fired at point-bank range through the crown of his skull, stopped the charge that had all but succeeded in reaching me, and he rolled back on to the sands of the Chinar, his career at an end.

Whistling on my way back to Sopathy, I gathered Ranga and Byra from the *muthee* trees on which they were sitting. Hearing my shots, and seeing my approach along the riverbed, they gathered I had killed the tiger.

Next morning we found him to be an average-sized, somewhat thin, male. My shot from beneath the cartwheel, fired seventeen days earlier, had done more damage than I had thought, for it had passed through his right shoulder, splintering the bone, and out again. But the wound was in good condition, and I have little doubt, would eventually have healed, although the tiger would have remained a cripple. My first shot of the night before had passed through his open mouth, and out through the neck, blowing a gaping hole. Still, he had come on. The second shot had gone high, entering behind the left shoulder, passing downwards through the lungs, and out again. And still he had come on. It was only my last shot, through the crown of his skull, that had shattered the brain that impelled his indomitable spirit.

What had made this tiger a man-eater? This is the riddle that every hunter tries to solve when he kills a man-eater, be it tiger or panther, not only for his own information, but for the education of the general public. And this beast proved to be no exception to the invariable rule that it is the human race itself that causes a tiger to become a man-eater. It had an old bullet wound in the same leg—the right —as had been injured by me in our first encounter, only lower down; embedded in the elbow joint was a flattened lead ball, fired from some musket or gun a year or more earlier.

This foreign body, embedded in that most important joint, had not only caused the tiger to suffer intense agony, but had greatly impeded his movements when it came to killing his legitimate food, wild game and cattle. It had weakened the use of the right leg, which plays an all-important part in gripping and pulling down his normal prey. Without a doubt, this was the sole factor that forced this tiger to turn to human beings as food, in order to keep himself from starving.

Two

Alam Bux and the Big Black Bear

THE STORY I AM NOW ABOUT TO RELATE CONCERNS A SLOTH BEAR. Quite a big, black and bad bear.

All bears, as I have had occasion to remark in other stories, are excitable, unreliable and bad-tempered animals. They have a reputation for attacking people without apparent reason, provided that person happens to pass too close, either while the bear is asleep or feeding, or just ambling along. So the natives give bears a wide berth; together with the elephant, they command the greatest respect of the jungle-dwelling folk.

This particular bear was exceptional among his kind for his unwarranted and exceptionally bad temper and aggressiveness. He would go out of his way to attack people, even when he saw them a long distance away.

The reason for his unusual conduct was difficult to explain. There were many stories about him, which were as varied as they were extraordinary. The most unpretentious was that he was quite mad. Other stories had it that he was a 'she' who had been robbed of her cubs and had sworn a vendetta against the human race. I think that the bear had been wounded or injured at some time by some human being. Perhaps the most fantastic of the stories was to the effect that this bear, almost a year previously, had kidnapped an Indian girl as a mate while she was grazing a flock of goats on the hill where he lived. The story went on to say that the whole village had turned out, *en masse*, to rescue the girl, which they had finally succeeded in doing, much to the bear's annoyance; he had then taken to attacking human beings in retaliation.

Whatever the reason be, this bear had quite a long list of victims to his credit; I was told that some twelve persons had been killed, and two dozen others injured.

Like all bears, he invariably attacked the face of the victim, which he commenced to tear apart with his tremendously long and powerful claws, in addition to biting viciously with deliberate intent to ensure the success of his handiwork. Quite half the injured had lost one or both eyes; some had lost their noses, while others had had their cheeks bitten through. Those who had been killed had died with their faces almost torn from their heads. Local rumours had it that the bear had also taken to eating his victims, the last three of whom had been partly devoured.

I had no opportunity to verify the truth of these rumours, but felt that they might be true to some extent, as the Indian sloth bear is a known devourer of carrion at times, although generally he is entirely vegetarian, restricting himself to roots, fruit, honey, white ants and similar delicacies. So fresh meat, even human meat, might not be unwelcome.

This bear originally lived in the Nagvara Hills, which lie to the east of the large town of Arsikere, some 105 miles northwest of Bangalore, and in Mysore State.

It was on these hills that he had perpetrated his earliest offences. Then, as he lost his fear of mankind and grew bolder, for no apparent reason he came down to the plains and commenced to harass people in their fields at dawn and dusk. He would come out from one or the other of the numerous small boulder-strewn hillocks that were dotted here and there, to forage for food.

I had been hearing occasional stories of this animal for about a year, but had not paid much attention to them, as I felt that, like nearly all the stories one hears in India of maulings and killings by wild animals, they were greatly exaggerated. Furthermore, as I think I have mentioned somewhere else, Bruin is quite an old friend of mine, against whom I have no antipathy. I was therefore most disinclined to go after him.

But there came an incident that made me do so. I have an old friend, an aged Muslim named Alam Bux, who is the guardian of a Mohammedan shrine situated on the main road which leads past Arsikere and on to Shimoga. This shrine is the burial place of a Mohammedan saint who lived some fifty years ago, and like hundreds of similar shrines scattered over the length and breadth of India, is preserved and held sacred by the Muslim community. Each shrine has its own guardian, or caretaker; invariably some old man who is quartered at the shrine itself to keep it clean and care for it. One of his particular duties is to light a lamp over the shrine, which is kept burning all night, to signify that the memory of the saint burns ever brightly in the bosoms of the faithful.

I first met Alam Bux on a dark night while motoring from Bangalore to Shimoga on my way to a tiger-hunt. The rear wheel of my Studebaker flew off, and the back brake-drum hit the road with a terrific jolt. I happened to be alone at the time and, stepping out of the car, viewed the situation with considerable disgust and annoyance. Fortunately for me, the incident had taken place almost opposite the shrine, and old Alam Bux, waking up at the noise made by the brake-drum striking and dragging along the road, came out to see what it was all about. Seeing my predicament, the old man volunteered to help me, which he did to a very considerable extent by bringing a lantern from his abode, gathering stones to serve as 'packing' while I raised the axle of the car, and last, but by no means least, by serving me with a bowl of hot tea. I thanked the old man, after he had replaced the truant wheel, and promised that I would look him up whenever I happened to pass his little hut again. This promise I had faithfully kept, and I never failed to bring the old man something, by way of supplies, on any occasion that I happened to pass.

Some four hundred yards beyond the shrine is a small knoll of heaped boulders, among which grew the usual lantana shrub. All around this knoll, and right up to the shrine and adjacent roadway, were fields in which the villagers grew groundnuts after the monsoon rains. Now, bears are very fond of groundnuts and our big black bear was no exception to this rule. The boulder-covered hillock offered a convenient lodging, and the groundnut fields were a great attraction. So he took up residence among the rocks.

He made his abode in a deep recess beneath an overhanging boulder. Hungry by sunset, he could be seen coming forth from his cave, and, as twilight deepened into nightfall, he would amble down the knoll and come out on to the groundnut fields. Here he would spend a busy night, eating, uprooting, and generally shuffling about over a wide area throughout the hours of the darkness. Early dawn would find him replete, with his belly full of roots and nuts, white ants, grubs and other miscellaneous fodder which he had come across during the hours of his foraging. Leisurely he would climb back to his abode, there to spend the hot hours of the day in deep and bearly slumber. I forgot to mention that a small tank, which is the Indian colloquial name for a natural lake, was conveniently situated on the other side of the hillock, so that our friend, this bad bear, wanted for nothing.

About this time the fig trees that bordered the main road which ran past the little shrine came into season, and their clusters of ripe red fruit filled the branches, spilling on to the ground beneath carpeting the earth in a soft, red, spongy mass. Hundreds of birds of all varieties fed on the figs during the day. At night, scores of flying fox, the large Indian fruitbat resembling in size and appearance the far-famed 'vampire' bat, would come in their numbers, flapping about with leathern wings, screeching, clawing and fighting among themselves as they gormandized the ripe fruit.

These numerous visitors, both by day and night, would knock down twice the number of figs they ate, which added to the profusion of fruit already lying scattered on the ground, blown down by the wind and often falling of their own weight. All this offered additional attraction to the bear, which now found a pleasing change to his menu. It was there in abundance, just waiting to be eaten.

So from the fields he would visit the fig trees, and thus his foraging brought him into the precincts of the shrine. That is how the trouble began.

Alam Bux had a son, a lad aged about twenty-two years, who, together with the guardian's aged wife and younger sister, lived at the shrine. One night the family had their meal at about nine, and were preparing to go to bed, when the boy for some reason went outside. It happened to be a dark night, and the bear also happened to be eating figs in the vicinity. Seeing the human figure suddenly appear, he felt that this was an unwarranted intrusion and immediately attacked the youth; more by accident than deliberately, the bear bit through the youth's throat and not the face, which was his usual first objective. The boy tried to scream, and had kicked and fought. The bear bit him again, this time through the nose and one eye, and clawed him severely across his chest, shoulders and back. Then it let him go and loped away into the darkness.

The boy staggered back to his parents streaming with blood. His jugular vein had been punctured, and although they had tried to staunch the bleeding with such rags as were available, they failed in their attempt to save his life, which ebbed away in the darkness, as cloth after cloth, and rag after rag, became soaked in his blood.

The false dawn witnessed the youth's passing while the old bear, replete with figs and groundnuts, climbed back to his cave among the boulders.

Alam Bux was a poor man and could not afford the money to send me a telegram, nor even his fare to Bangalore, either by train or by bus. But he sent me a postcard on which was scrawled the sad story; it was written in pencil, in shaky Urdu script. It was stained with the tears of his sorrow. The postcard arrived two days later, and I left for Asikere within three hours.

I had anticipated that the shooting of this bear would be an easy matter and that it would take an hour or two at the most. Therefore, I did not go prepared for a long trip. I carried just my torch, .405 Winchester rifle, and a single change of clothing. I reached Alam Bux shortly after five in the evening and it did not take him long to tell me his story.

There was no moonlight at this time. Nevertheless the plan to be followed seemed a simple one; namely, to wait till it grew quite dark and then set forth to search for the bear with the aid of my torch.

With this procedure in view, Alam Bux allowed me inside his abode by sunset, and closed the door to give the appearance that all was quiet. In the dingy little room we chatted in the flickering light of a small oil lamp, while he repeatedly lamented the death of his son. In fact, within a few minutes the whole family were weeping and wailing. I had, perforce, to listen to this continuously till eight, when I could stand it no longer and decided to go out in search of the bear.

Loading my rifle, and seeing that the torch was functioning properly, I stepped outside, Alam Bux closing and bolting his door behind me. The darkness was intense, and as I pressed the switch of the torch fixed near the muzzle of the rifle, its bright beams shone forth over the groundnut fields to my left, and the dense aisle of fig trees bordering the road to my right.

The bear was nowhere in sight and so I started to look for him, beginning with the fig trees. These trees grew on both sides of the road, so I judged the best thing to do would be to walk along the road itself, swinging my rifle from one side of the road to the other. I walked in this fashion away from Asikere for about a mile and a half, but saw no signs of the bear. I then walked back to the shrine and continued in the opposite direction for another mile and a half, but there were still no signs of the bear. So I came back to the shrine, and started to search the groundnut fields.

Bright glimmers of various pairs of eyes glared back at me, reflected by the torch beam. But they proved to be those of rabbits and three or four jackals. I circumvented the hillock and walked along the margin of the tank on the other side; where I came across a small sounder of wild pigs wallowing in the mud. But still no sign of the old bear was to be seen. I then walked closer to the foot of the knoll, and around it two or three times, shining my light upwards and in all directions. It was a tiring work, and the old bear did not put in his appearance. On the third occasion I almost stepped upon a very large Russell's viper that was coiled between two rocks in my direct *path*. Engaged as I was, looking for the reflecting gleam of the bear's eyes, I did not watch the ground before me. My foot was within a few inches of the viper when he inflated his body with a loud, rasping hiss, preparatory to striking. Instinctively I heeded his warning not to come any nearer and leapt backwards, at the same time shining the torch directly upon the snake, which lunged forth with jaws apart to bite the spot where, just a moment before, my legs had been. It was a narrow shave, and for the moment I felt like shooting the viper. But that would have caused a tremendous disturbance and might frighten away the bear, in addition to wasting a valuable cartridge. After all, the snake had been good enough to warn me, and so, in return, I threw a small stone at it, which caused it to slither away beneath the rocks.

By this time it was evident that the bear had either gone out earlier in the evening and wandered far away, or else he was not hungry and was still in his cave. I returned to Alam Bux's shack and decided to make another tour in a couple of hours.

This I did, and made two further tours after that, making four in all, but the bear was not to be seen, and the false dawn found me still vainly circling the hillock in search of the enemy.

With daylight, I told Alam Bux that I would return to Bangalore but he begged me to stay for the day and to climb the hill and search the cave for the bear. In the meantime his wife had prepared some hot *'chappaties'*—round flat cakes made from wheat flour—and a dish of steaming tea, both of which I consumed with relish. Then I fell asleep. At about noon Alam Bux woke me, to say that his wife had prepared special 'pillao rice' in my honour. Thanking him for this, I tucked into it too, and in a very short time polished off the lot. Mrs. Alam Bux appeared highly gratified that I so relished her cooking. The sun was now at its meridian and shone mercilessly on the rocks which blazed and shimmered in the noon-day heat. It would be a good time to look for the bear, I knew, assuming he was at home, as he would be fast asleep.

Alam Bux came with me up the hill and from a distance of fifty yards pointed out the shelving rock beneath which the bear had its cave. I clambered upwards on tiptoe, the rubber soles of my shoes making no sound on the rocks. But against this advantage I was soon to feel a greater disadvantage, as the heat from the sun-baked stone penetrated the rubber and began to burn the soles of my feet.

Coming up to the entrance of the cave, I squatted on my haunches and listened attentively.

Now a sleeping bear invariably snores, often as loud as does a human being. If the bear was fast asleep, as I hoped he would be, I counted upon hearing that tell-tale sound. But no sound greeted my ear, and after sitting thus for almost ten minutes, the sun began making itself felt through the back of my shirt. Some pebbles lay at hand and, picking up a few, I began to throw them into the cave.

Now such a procedure is calculated to make any sleeping bear very angry. But I could still hear nothing. So I went closer to the entrance and threw the stones right inside. Still nothing happened. I threw more stones, but again with negative results. The bear was not in his cave.

Descending the hill, I told Alam Bux the news and announced my intention to return to Bangalore, asking him to send me a telegram if the bear put in a further appearance. I gave him some money, both for the cost of the telegram and to tide him over immediate expenses. Then I left for Bangalore. A month elapsed, and I heard nothing more.

About twenty miles across country, and in a northwesterly direction from where the shrine is situated, the forest of Chikmagalur, in the Kadur district of Mysore, begins. About halfway between Chikmagalur and Kadur stands the small town of Sakrepatna, surrounded by the jungle.

The next news that came to me was that a bear had seriously mauled two woodcutters near Sakrepatna, one of whom had later died. The district Forest Officer (D.F.O) of Chikmagalur wrote to me, asking if I would come and shoot this bear.

I concluded that it was the same bear that had been the cause of the death of Alam Bux's son, but to look for one particular bear in the wide range of forest was something like searching for the proverbial needle in a haystack, and so I wrote back to the D.F.O. to try and get more exact information as to the whereabouts of the animal.

After ten days he replied that the bear was said to be living in a cave on a hillock some three miles from the town, near the footpath leading to a large lake known as the 'Ionkere' also that it had since mauled the Forest Guard, who had been walking along this *path* on his regular beat.

So I motored to Chikmagalur, picked up the D.F.O., and proceeded to the town of Sakrepatna, where there is a small rest house owned by the Mysore Forest department. Here I set up my headquarters for the next few days.

As luck would have it—or bad luck, if you call it that—the very next afternoon a man came running to the bungalow, to tell us that a cattle grazier—his brother in fact—had been grazing his cattle in the vicinity of the very hill where the bear was supposed to be living, when he had been attacked by the animal. He had screamed for help, and his cries had been mingled with the growls of the bear. His brother, who was lower down the hill and nearer the footpath, hearing the sounds had waited no longer, but had fled back to the bungalow to bring us the news.

Now bears are essentially nocturnal animals never moving about during daylight. At most, they may be met with at dusk or early dawn, but certainly not in the afternoon. Probably the unfortunate grazier had strayed too close to some spot where the bear had been sleeping, causing it to attack him at that unusual time. That could be the only reason for this strange attack.

It was nearing 4.30 p.m. when he brought us this news, and I set forth with my rifle and torch and three or four helpers to try to rescue the grazier who had been attacked. We soon found that the distance to the spot was much greater than we had been told by the unfortunate man's brother. I figured I had walked nearly six miles into the jungle before we came to the foot of a hill that was densely covered with scrub, including clumps of bamboo. It was then nearly six and, being winter, it was getting dark. The men I had brought along refused to come farther, and said that they would return to Sakrepatna, advising me to accompany them and suggesting that we should go back next morning to continue our search. The brother of the missing man volunteered to wait where we stood, but was too fearful to come farther into the jungle. The most he could do to help me in finding his missing relative was vaguely to indicate, with a wave of his arm, the general area where the attack had occurred.

I went forward in that direction, calling loudly the name of the man who had been mauled. There was no answer to my shouts, and I advanced deeper and deeper into the scrub. By this time it was almost dark, but I did not feel perturbed, as I had brought my torch and began to flash it about as I sought a way through the undergrowth.

Soon it became so dense that I could make no further progress, and was on the point of turning back, when I thought I heard a faint moan, away in the distance. The ground at this point sloped downwards into a sort of valley that lay between two ridges of the hill, and the moan seemed to come from somewhere in the recesses of this valley.

The missing man's name was Thimma, and, cupping both hands to my mouth, I shouted this name lustily, waiting every now and then to listen for a reply. Yes! There, undoubtedly, it was again! A moaning cry, feeble, but nevertheless audible. It definitely came to me from the valley.

Forcing my way through the thickets, I struggled down the decline, slipping on rocks and loose stones, catching myself every now and then on the thorns. After a couple of hundred yards of such progress, I called again. After some time I heard a moaning answer, somewhere to my right. I proceeded in this fashion, following the cry till I eventually found Thimma, lying at the foot of a tree in a puddle of his own blood. His face was a mass of raw flesh and broken bones, and the only way of distinguishing that he was breathing was by the bubbles of air that forced themselves through the clotting blood. In addition, the bear had raked him across the stomach with its claws, tearing open the outer flesh, so that a loop of intestine protruded. He was hardly conscious when I found him, and I soon realised that what I had taken to be a moaning reply to my calls were just the groans he kept making, every now and then, in his delirium.

The situation was critical, and after examination I saw that another night's exposure would cause him to die by morning. There was therefore no alternative but to carry him back to the spot where I had left his brother. Lifting him on to my shoulder was a tricky business, in the terrible state that he was in. To make matters worse, he was a heavily built man, equal to myself in weight. But I managed to lift him and, using my rifle butt as a prop, began to struggle upwards the way I had come.

I never wish to experience again so terrible a journey. I had almost gained the ridge down which I had lately come when the accident occurred. My left foot slipped and came down heavily between two boulders. There was a sharp, shooting, wrenching pain as I collapsed on the rock with Thimma on top of me, while the rifle clattered to the ground.

I had sprained my ankle, and was now myself unable to walk. From where we lay, I began to shout to the brother; but after nearly an hour I realised he either could not or would not hear me. There was no alternative but to spend the night with the dying man.

Desiring to make the torch batteries last the night, if that were possible, I refrained from using them more than was necessary. The early hours of morning became bitterly cold and Thimma's groans became more and more feeble, till eventually they turned into a gurgle. I realised he was dying. At about 5 a.m. he died, and there I sat beside him till daylight eventually came, shortly after six.

I then made a determined effort to drag myself to my feet, but found my leg would not support my weight. I tried to crawl, but the thorns formed an impenetrable barrier. They tore my hands, my face and my clothing to shreds. I soon gave it up and became reconciled to the fact that I would have to wait till a rescue party came to search for us.

It was well past noon before the Forest department people, accompanied by Thimma's brother and a dozen villagers, came anywhere near the scene. Eventually, guided by my shouts, they located us, and that evening I was back at

ALAM BUX AND THE BIG BLACK BEAR

Sakrepatna forest bungalow, lying on the cot with an immensely swollen ankle. The D.F.O. turned up at about nine o'clock and drove me in my car to Chikmagalur, where I went to the local hospital for treatment. It was a week before I managed to hobble around. You may guess that by this time I was extremely angry with myself at the delay, and more so with the big, bad, black bear that had caused all the trouble. I was determined that I would get him at any cost, just as soon as I could walk.

In the meantime he had not been idle, but had mauled two more men who had been walking along the *path* to the lonkere Lake.

Four days later saw me back at Sakrepatna, just about able to walk, although not for long distances. Here I was told that the bear had taken to visiting some fields about a mile from the village, bordered by *boram* trees, the fruit of which was just then coming into season. At 5 p.m. I reached the trees in question and, selecting the largest, which had the most fruit, decided to spend the night at its foot, hoping that the bear showed up. I sat on the ground with my back to the trunk, my rifle across my knees.

Shortly after eleven I heard the grunting, grumbling sound of an approaching bear. He stopped frequently, no doubt to pick up some morsel, and as he came closer I heard the scratching sounds he made in digging for roots. He took nearly an hour to reach the *boram* tree, by which time I was amply prepared. Finally, he broke cover and ambled into the open, a black blob silhouetted in the faint glimmer of the stars.

I pressed the torch switch and the beams fell on him. He rose on his hind legs to regard me with surprise, and I planted my bullet in his chest between the arms of the white V-mark that showed clearly in the torchlight. And that was the end of that really bad bear.

MAN-EATERS AND JUNGLE KILLERS

Bears, as a rule, are excitable but generally harmless creatures. This particular bear carried the mark of Cain, in that he had become the wanton and deliberate murderer of several men, whom he had done to death in the most terrible fashion, without provocation.

Three

The Mamandur Man-Eater

THIS ANIMAL WAS A FEMALE, AND YOUNG AT THAT; SO THERE WAS apparent reason for her becoming a man-killer. But beca she began her depredations shortly after the death of the m eating tiger of the Chamala Valley—whose career I have t in the story entitled 'The Striped Terror of the Cham Valley'*—and operated partly in the same locality, there were perhaps some grounds for the local gossip that set her down as the mate of that august killer. Another, and equally likely explanation, was that she was a grown-up cub, who had learned the evil practice of man-killing and man-eating from her evil sire.

Whatever her antecedents, this tigress made her first attempt at killing a human being when she attacked a herdsman, who attempted to succour a fine milch-cow, which she had

---

* See the author's earlier book, *Nine Man-Eaters and one Rogue*.

chosen to attack from amongst his herd of cattle, and whose neck she had just skilfully broken. The herdsman very bravely but foolishly attempted to frighten the tigress away from the fallen cow by shouting and brandishing his staff in the air. Mostly such tactics have the desired effect of frightening the tiger away, but in this case the effect was just the reverse. Instead of bounding away, the tigress bounded towards the herdsman, covering the short twenty yards that separated them at incredible speed. The herdsman turned tail and bolted, but the tigress dealt him a raking blow with her front paw that opened the flesh from shoulder to buttocks. The weight of the blow bore him to the ground; but in this, her first attack on a human being, the tigress apparently considered she had inflicted enough damage, for she turned back to the cow she had just killed.

With returning consciousness, the herdsman could hear the crunch of bones a mere forty yards away as the tigress fed on the cow. Fortunately, this man kept his head and did not attempt to get to his feet. In all probability any such movement would have provoked a second, and this time fatal, attack.

So he lay as he had fallen, on his face, but by stealthily moving his head very slowly and slightly, he was able to see the tigress as she fed.

He told me afterwards that he would never forget the next hour for the rest of his life. Apparently, the tigress stopped eating every now and then, raised her head and glanced in his direction. Once she got to her feet and even took a few steps towards him. The poor fellow almost screamed with terror, and nearly made the mistake of moving. Perhaps his very terror saved his life by making him incapable of movement. Fortunately, the tigress then changed her mind and returned to the cow.

THE MAMANDUR MAN-EATER

It was more than an hour, the herdsman told me, before the tigress eventually decided she had eaten enough. She then leisurely sat on her haunches, licked her forepaws thoroughly and began to clean her face. With a final backward glance at his recumbent figure, she at last got to her feet, stretched herself contentedly and walked off into the jungle.

The herdsman lay still for another ten minutes, to make perfectly sure she had really gone. Then he got to his feet and dashed homewards as fast as he could run.

There is at least one other, equally remarkable, end to this story: the deep scratches the tigress had inflicted healed completely in spite of the absence of any proper medical treatment, apart from some crushed herbs, mixed with cow-dung, which the native doctor rubbed into the wounds. Perhaps the shawl he had been wearing, draped across his shoulders, had prevented the poisonous matter under the claws from entering the bloodstream.

This incident had occurred scarcely four miles from Mamandur railway station, where a rocky escarpment fell sharply for about three hundred feet into a forest glen, through which ran a little stream.

The next incident was also one of mauling, but this time the victim was not so lucky. Again it was a cowherd who was involved, an elderly man who died of his wounds. The events were much the same as in the earlier case. The tigress had dashed into a herd of cattle that was grazing a mile to the west of the railway line that cut through the forest, and had once more selected a milch-cow for her victim. As the frightened cattle stampeded past the elderly herdsman, he ran in the direction from which they had come to learn the cause of their alarm.

Soon he came upon the tigress, astride the dead cow. This time no attempt was made to frighten her off; the herdsman just stopped in his track in surprise. But evidently the tigress resented his appearance on the scene, for she attacked and mauled him severely. Then she walked back to the dead cow and dragged it away into the undergrowth.

It was three hours before help came to the old man. The cattle had stampeded across the railway line. The old man's brother, coming in search of him, saw that the cattle had moved and that their owner was nowhere to be seen. Standing on the railway embankment, he called loudly to his brother, but got no response. Then sensing that something was wrong, he hurried back to Mamandur village for help.

The search party, following the tracks of the stampeding cattle, came upon the mauled man. He was unconscious and almost dead from loss of blood. They carried him to the village and then to the station, intending to put him in the guard's van of a goods train that was due in half-an-hour, bound for the town of Renigunta, nine miles away, where there was a hospital. But the old herdsman died before the goods train reached Mamandur.

Only at her third killing did this tigress develop man-eating tendencies. She again attacked a herdsman, on this occasion at about nine in the morning. How it happened was related by a second herdsman, who was standing beside the first at the time of the attack. The tigress dashed out amongst the herd as usual and leapt upon a young bull. Somehow, she failed in her initial attempt to bring the bull down. On the other hand, the bull, with the tigress on his back, dashed madly to where the two herdsmen were standing. One of them—the man who lived to tell the tale—bolted. The other just did nothing, but appeared to be rooted to the spot with surprise.

The fleeing man looked back only once, in time to see the tigress leap from the bolting bull on to the terror-stricken

THE MAMANDUR MAN-EATER

herdsman. He saw no more, for the very good reason that he turned away and ran as fast and as far from the spot as he could.

When the rescue party turned up some hours later, armed with sticks and matchlocks, the body of the victim was not to be seen. So the party went back for reinforcements. Another three hours elapsed before the rescuers, now numbering nearly a hundred men, arrived at the scene of the attack. They followed a clear trail and found the corpse, lying on its face in the sandy bed of a narrow *nullah*. A part of the chest and buttocks had been eaten.

Three further human kills followed during the next couple of months. Of these, one was a herdsman, one a traveller on the Renigunta road, and the third a Lumbani, who had gone out to gather wild honey. Thereafter, all cattle-grazing stopped, as did also the collection of wild honey. No more travellers dared to come by road on foot. They came by train instead.

Mr. Littlewood, the district Forest Officer at the time, wrote to me, suggesting I might spend a few days at the beautiful Forest Bungalow at Mamandur and try to bag this tigress. With fifteen days' privilege leave to my credit, I caught the night mail-train from Bangalore; but it was 3.30 p.m. next day before I alighted from a slow passenger train at the little wayside station of Mamandur.

The forest bungalow lies a bare seven furlongs away on the top of a small hillock. The *path* to the bungalow traverses the small village of Mamandur, where I stopped for some time to make it widely known that I had come especially to shoot the tigress. My object was to get the news to spread from mouth to mouth, so that I would not only pick up all available known details about the animal, but, more particularly, would be acquainted with the news of any fresh kills that took place, either animal or human. I also negotiated the purchase of three buffalow heifers, which I paid for in cash, placing them in the charge of the local *shikari*, a man by the name of Arokiaswamy, whom I had engaged on earlier visits to Mamandur.

The bungalow had a wide and well-sheltered verandah. From its hillock fire-lines, or 'forest-lines' as they are sometimes called, radiated in five directions. Those south and south-westwards ran close to the village and railway embankment respectively. The other three struck far into the forest, and the eye could travel along them for many miles. The fire-line to the north stretched away towards the escarpment where the very first herdsman had been mauled by the tigress. Those to the east and southeast travelled in almost straight lines into the labyrinth of the jungle, like the spokes of some giant wheel. The country in both these directions was flat.

In years gone by, when game was far more plentiful, I had spent many a pleasant early morning or late evening, standing on the verandah or on the plinth of the bungalow with a pair of powerful binoculars, looking along those forest-lines. It was very common to see sambar, spotted deer and peafowl cross from one side to another. I had seen bear on three occasions, early in the morning, and a tiger crossing the northern fire-line at five in the evening. Also, although quite two miles away, I had witnessed a pack of eleven wild dogs 'ringing' an old bear. I had dashed after them on that occasion—to save the bear from the cruel fate that awaited it—arriving just as the eleven demons closed on the harried, exhausted, but brave, old beast. Three of the dogs lay dead before they realised they had to deal with a new foe. A fourth tumbled to the crack of my rifle as the pack began to run away, and a fifth joined the other four by the time the remnants of the pack were out of sight in the jungle.

I was using my old .405 Winchester rifle in those days, and had emptied my magazine. Only then did I realise I had to face a maddened bear, who had been infuriated by the dogs and the pain of the bites he had already received.

He was then about sixty yards away, and he charged straight at me, screaming, 'Woof! Woof!' I ran as fast as I could along the forest-line, and as I did so I opened the under-lever action of the .405, rammed home a cartridge in the breach, and closed the lever, which automatically cocked the rifle. Whipping around I faced the bear, which was scarcely fifteen yards away. In true bear style, when five yards away, he rose on his hind legs to deliver the final 'coup de grâce', which is popularly thought to be that most fearsome of caresses, 'a bear's hug', of which we have all heard so much.

Actually, the south Indian sloth bear does not 'hug' his adversary. He rises on his hind legs to tear at his victim's face with his formidable, three-inch long talons, or to bite him on the head with his powerful teeth. In rising to his hind legs, the bear exposed the broad white V-mark that all sloth bears carry on their chests. With the one cartridge I had in the rifle, I shot him in the base of the V. He fell forward and lay still, just two yards away!

Three of the wild dogs had been males, the other two were females. The forest department paid me a reward of ten rupees for each male and fifteen rupees for each bitch. As wild dogs are very destructive to deer, their shooting is encouraged. I was sorry to have had to kill old Bruin, but he brought it on himself.

All this had happened very, very long ago.

Another factor that made this bungalow very attractive was the sea breeze that blew in from the east shortly after two o' clock each afternoon. I think, as the crow flies, the Bay of Bengal is not less than seventy-five miles from this little bungalow; and I am no authority to argue about the distance at which a sea breeze ceases to be effective. I only know that, at almost two each afternoon it turns the verandah of that little bungalow into a delightfully cool spot on which to take a nap. If you don't believe me, visit Mamandur Forest Bungalow.

It was too late that evening to tie out more than one of the three buffaloes, which only arrived at 5.30 p.m. This buffalow I took for two miles along the northern fire-line, where I tied it at the foot of a large and leafy tamarind tree. It was past seven when I got back, so I kept the other two buffaloes in the garage and asked Arokiaswamy to sleep in the kitchen.

Early next morning we were astir. First we took the bait which we had tied two miles away the previous night, and which was still alive, right up to the foot of the escarpment where the very first attack had taken place. There we secured it to the roots of a tree in a beautiful glade of rank, green grass.

We came back to the bungalow and took the second heifer along the fire line stretching to the east, where I tied it at almost the very spot where my encounter with the wild dogs and the bear had taken place.

Returning for the second time to the bungalow, we took the third and last heifer across the railway line to the west, and tied it near the spot where the elderly herdsman had been killed.

It was past midday when I got back to the bungalow for the third time, and blazing hot too. Taking off my sweat-soaked shirt, I ate a belated cold lunch and awaited the advent of the sea breeze, which I knew would start at about two. Nor was I disappointed; for when it began, it turned that broiling-hot verandah to the likeness of the shores of some far-distant South Sea Island, where we read that 'the sea-breezes forever play'.

The next two days were uninteresting. I visited all three baits each day, but none of them had been touched. The evening of the fifth day brought a tragedy.

THE MAMANDUR MAN-EATER

The semaphores along the railway lines of southern India are lit at night by kerosene oil lamps, except in the shunting yards of the larger railway junctions. As you are no doubt aware, every ordinary railway station has two sets of signals on each side of it; the near or 'home' signal, and a more distant, or 'outer' signal, as it is called. Normally, the kerosene oil lamps at these signals are cleaned, trimmed, refilled and lit by a pointsman or an other railway employee appointed for the purpose who does his job at about six each evening. But owing to the presence of the tigress at Mamandur, and the fact that the outer signals, both in the direction of Renigunta to the south and Setigunta to the northwest, were surrounded by forest, it had become the custom to light these lamps well before five, while the sun was still up.

That evening two pointsmen had set out on this task at 4 p.m., one walking towards Renigunta, and the other in the opposite direction. The second man never came back.

Shortly before six a body of seven men came rushing to the forest bungalow, sent by the stationmaster, to tell me what had happened. Hastily grabbing my rifle, torch and a few other necessities for a nightlong vigil, I sent the seven men back to the station, and Arokiaswamy along with them, as he absolutely refused to stay in the bungalow alone that night. Then I hurried up the forest-line that led to the west, which I knew met the railway track almost midway between the 'inner' and 'outer' signals.

When I reached the railway line, which here ran along an embankment ten feet high, I looked to my left and saw the 'inner' signal, with its red light twinkling.

'Stupid man', I thought. 'Instead of attending to the outer light first, while it was still early, and coming back to the inner on his way to the station, he wasted time on the inner light, and then went to the outer, when it was considerably later.'

Turning to the right, I walked along the embankment towards the 'outer' semaphore, which came into view when I turned a corner. As I walked, I looked along and about the tracks for signs of the attack that must have taken place while the pointsman was approaching the outer signal. I found nothing. Then I came to the foot of the 'outer', and looked up. The light was burning!

So the man had been attacked on his way back after he had attended to the 'outer' signal, and not before. Added to this was the fact that the light of the 'inner' signal was also burning. Perhaps he had not attended to that light first, as I had originally thought. Perhaps he had lit the outer, then the inner, and had been attacked somewhere between the inner signal and the station yard.

But was that likely in view of the fact that all the area from the station up to the 'inner' signal, and even a little beyond it, was open cultivated land? Would any tiger, even if it was a man-eater, walk about thus boldly on absolutely open land in broad, daylight? It was possible, but rather unlikely.

My watch showed 6.55 p.m., and it was rapidly growing dark as I began to retrace my steps towards the inner signal, keeping now a sharper lookout than ever. An early moon had risen, which was indeed fortunate, or it would have become quite dark by this time.

Almost at the spot where I had first come on to the embankment from the forest-line was a small culvert, crossing a narrow but deep *nullah*. Something white there caught my eye, fluttering between the sleepers of the railway track as it spanned this *nullah*. I stopped, and peered between the sleepers.

It was the white *dhoti* worn by the railwayman. Wedged under a boulder, twenty feet away and clear of the embankment, lay an elongated, dark shape, which I knew to be the body of the victim. Even in that uncertain light I could tell that the body had been partly devoured in the short time that had elapsed since the kill had taken place. The neck had been bitten through, and the head lay about a yard away. Because the tigress might perhaps be in the vicinity at that moment, or even watching me from the cover of the bushes, it would be unnecessarily dangerous to descend the embankment and make a closer examination of the body.

A hasty survey of the position made me decide to lie at right angles across the railway lines and exactly in the middle of the culvert. I would thus be safe from attack from the front or rear, as to do this the tigress would have to leap a clear fifteen from the bottom of the *nullah* on to the track. This left her the choice of attacking me along the track, either to my right or left. I should have told you that the span of the culvert was about twenty feet. Not much, but it would at least give me time to see the tigress.

Of course, there was the possibility that she would creep up at an angle to the embankment and attack me obliquely, either from the front, or worse still, from behind; and either to the left or right of me.

It was a chance that had to be taken.

I had already clamped my torch to the rifle walking from the bungalow. I placed my haversack beneath my chest, to soften contact with the rail. This section of track was broad gauge, which means that the lines were five feet six inches apart. By spreading my legs widely, I found my soles just touched the other rail and did not overlap it. The teak—weed 'sleeper', on which I lay, was perhaps eight inches wide: not over-comfortable to lie on and awfully hard!

The moon was shining brightly by this time and lit the scene clearly. The corpse and its severed head were clearly visible against the lighter colour of the rock and the finely-grained white sand of the *nullah* in which it lay. Everything was deathly silent.

The red light glimmered from the friendly inner signal; it seemed to remind me that help was close—but yet so distant.

The hours ticked by; a sambar stag belled from the jungle to the west. Perhaps that call heralded that the tigress was on the move! No, for it was answered by another stag, further away to the northeast, and then by another to the east. Periodically, the spotted deer also gave vent to their sharp cries of alarm, 'Aiow! Aiow! Aiow!'

But the cries did not come from any one direction; if they had done so, that would have indicated definitely that some carnivore was afoot in that area. They came from all sides, far and near, indicating that several carnivores were on the move. Also, being a brilliant moonlight night, it was possible that packs of wild dogs were on the hunt. These animals chase their prey by day and never on a dark night, but on brilliant moonlit nights, in certain jungles, they occasionally reverse their habit and hunt by moonlight.

At midnight silence reigned again. And then the hair at the back of my neck began to rise, for what I was witnessing was eerie indeed. The severed head had rolled on to its side!

All this time it had been staring heavenwards; now its lifeless eyes and face were turned to me. Yet no animal had touched it, for it lay in the open, clearly visible in the bright moonlight.

I felt myself tremble and grow cold. I licked my dry lips and stared at that terrible head.

Again it moved! It had tried to roll back to its former position; it had turned halfway and then, as if it lacked the strength to complete the move, it had rolled back again and was staring me in the face.

THE MAMANDUR MAN-EATER

Now I may tell you I am a very practical person, not superstitious, nor afraid of the dark. I had spent many a night in a similar or even more dangerous position; I had sat over half-eaten human bodies before, and on earlier occasions I had imagined that I had seen them move. But never before in my life had I seen a severed human head actually turn around of its own accord, then try to turn back again and fail; finally, to roll back in obvious despair.

I almost cried out and for quite a while was seized with a powerful urge to get up and run towards the twinkling, friendly red light of the 'inner' signal. Then common sense reasserted itself. A dead head, human or otherwise, cannot move of its own accord. Something must have moved it!

I stared at the head intently, and the bright moonlight showed me the answer to my problem. Two black objects could be seen moving in the white sand. They were 'rhinoceros beetles': large insects, more than an inch-and-a-half long, with great spikes on their noses resembling the horn of a rhinoceros, from which resemblance they had got their name. Generally they are nocturnal, although one frequently sees them on forest roads, early in the morning, and again late at evening, busily rolling a ball of cow-dung, perhaps thrice their own size, to some unknown destination.

These two little creatures by their combined strength had succeeded in rolling this head over once, but the second time they had not quite succeeded. I had been so absorbed by what I saw that I had forgotten all about the tigress; she could easily have surprised me at that time.

It was now 1.40 and the rail beneath my chest began to tremble. Then I heard a distant rumbling sound which gradually grew louder and nearer. A sharp whistle rent the air and soon the brilliant headlight of an engine fell full upon me. It was the Night Mail from Madras to Bomaby.

Stiffly I got to my feet, lifted my haversack, walked to the end of the culvert, and then a couple of foot down the embankment. But I had entirely forgotten to take into account the vigilance of the driver of the train. He had clearly seen me in the bright headlight of the engine, although he had not noticed my rifle. As he was to tell me in a few minutes, he took me for a would-be suicide, deliberately lying on the track in order to be run over, whose courage had failed him at the last moment. I may mention, incidentally, that this method of committing suicide is rather popular in India.

Anyhow, with a grinding of brakes and violent hissing of steam, the train drew up just after the engine had passed me. The next thing I heard was the loud thudding of boots on the hard ground as figures ran towards me. It was the driver and his two firemen from the engine.

They charged up and grabbed me. Only then did they realise that I was obviously not what they had taken me to be. In the meantime, heads popped out of carriage windows, and a hundred voices began to question and conjecture. The guard came up from the rear with his bulls-eye lantern. So I had no alternative but to tell them what I was doing.

'Where is the man who has been eaten by the tiger?' asked the driver, a middle-aged Anglo-Indian. I pointed the corpse out to him. 'And you have been lying here in the open by yourself since evening?' he asked, incredulously.

When I replied in the affirmative, he added, very simply, 'You are quite mad,' and tapped his forehead significantly. His two firemen, and the Indian guard of the train, nodded heartily in agreement.

A few minutes later, the Mail puffed onwards, on its long journey to Bombay, and I was left alone once more. But I had little hope of the tigress putting in her appearance after so great a disturbance.

THE MAMANDUR MAN-EATER

At 2.30 a.m. the rails began to rumble again. This time I lay flat on the embankment, hiding my rifle, before the engine's headlight betrayed my presence. As a result, the goods train passed me by without stopping. At 4 a.m. again the rails rumbled and trembled, and I hid once more. It was the return Mail, from Bombay to Madras, that thundered by at full speed, as mail trains do not halt at Mamandur.

The false dawn came and went. The distant call of awakening peafowl fell on the air, as they cried, 'Mia-a-oo-Aaow' across the forest valleys to be answered by the cheery 'Whe-e-e-Kuch-Kaya Kaya-Khuck'm' of that most lovely bird, the grey junglecock.

A pale shell-pink tinted the sky above the eastern hills that stood sharply outlined now in velvety black. Meanwhile, the moon, which had held sway all night and was now about to set, began losing some of her brilliance.

In the east the shell-pink turned marvellously to mauve, then to a deep rose, tinged at its edges by the palest of greens and the purest of blues. The rose became orange-purple then orange alone, then deep red, and finally flame, as the glowing tip of the sun peeped above the wave-like lines of hilltops to the east.

Radiating beams of sunlight, cast heavenwards by that rapidly growing orb, touched the racing, fleecy clouds in the sky with all the colours of the spectrum. Then, suddenly, just as a butterfly bursts forth from its chrysalis, the sun surmounted the hills, driving before her, in eddying swirls, the wisps of mist from the damp jungle below.

It was another day, and to welcome its birth a glad chorus of song burst from the birds of the forest all around me. Every bush and tree throbbed with life, fresh, clean and new. Those who have seen the marvel of an Indian jungle sunrise will never forget it.

The head still stared up at me, but it was still now; the two rhinoceros beetles that had worked so diligently throughout the night had long since abandoned the unequal task and gone to rest.

I made my way to the station, disappointed and slowly, to tell the stationmaster he could allow the relations of the dead men to remove the remains for cremation, and by eight I was asleep on the verandah of the bungalow. In the afternoon the sea-breeze lulled me to a deeper slumber.

At 4 p.m. I awoke, feeling refreshed and fit, and ate a quick lunch-cum-tea, while listening to Arokiaswamy's report that he, with four others, had visited all the baits and had found them alive. It certainly looked as if this tigress was not going to kill any of the heifers I had tied out.

Then came sunset and bright moonlight. I felt like taking a walk. If I kept to the centre of any one of those five radiating forest fire-lines, I felt I would be safe enough, provided I maintained a sharp watch while I walked. There was also the definite chance of attracting the tigress, should our trails cross during the night.

I dressed for the occasion. In my own kit I had only khaki clothes and a black shirt which was useful for night *machan* work. So I went with Arokiaswamy to his hut, where I slipped on a long white shirt, allowing the shirttails to flutter loosely outside my khaki pants. Arokiaswamy further completed the disguise by tying a white turban round my head.

I did not know what the tigress would take me for if we met; but I know I was a source of considerable amusement to the villagers, who were somewhat shocked to hear of my plan.

I debated for a moment which fire-line to walk up first and decided to follow the one leading in the easterly direction. It was 7.30 p.m. when I started to walk. I kept in the centre of the line, and as I moved I allowed my eyes to rove freely around and about the bushes and undergrowth on both sides. Occasionally I glanced backwards.

Although the moonlight was brilliant, the bushes cast long black shadows, and clumps of thorns and grass looked ghostly grey around me. I realised that, for all the moonlight, my eyes could never pick out a lurking carnivore in that unreal sheen, even if it showed itself, which it would not. I should have to rely on my sense of hearing—and that other, my sixth sense!

At ten-minute intervals I whistled a bar of some tune or other to advertise my presence to the tigress; but only for half-a-minute at a time, so as not to impede my own ears, that were attuned to catch the slightest sound.

Thus, many a subtle rustle did I hear in the grassy hillocks as I passed them. Invariably, the nocturnal bamboo-rat was the culprit, as he scampered for cover at my approach. Then an indefinable, prolonged, slithering rustle: that was a snake, probably a Russell's viper, coiling comfortably around and around himself in the grass, to be cosy and warm. Something heavy descended from the sky, neatly on the back of a hare as it scampered across the fire-line. The hare squealed, and the great horned owl, which had attacked it, pecked it sharply on the forehead. I approached the owl, which extended both its wings to the ground to hide the hare from me, much in the same way as does a hen with chickens. I approached closer and the owl glowered; I drew closer still and the owl flew away. I picked up the limp hare and rubbed its back briskly. With regaining consciousness, it began to kick vigorously. I let it go into the long grass.

There were no bison in these jungles, nor elephants, but in their stead bear were plentiful. Nor was it long before I came upon Bruin, engaged in his favourite pastime of sucking white ants out of their hills. A distant sound, midway between a buzzing and a humming, a queer noise rather like someone inflating a bagpipe, or the sound of angry swarming bees, first told me that a bear was afoot. It grew louder and louder and was punctuated by grunts, coughs, whimpers of impatience and growls of annoyance.

There, to one side of the line and to my right was a white-ant hill. There standing up against it, with its head inside a hole, was a shaggy, black shape. It was the bear, blowing, sucking, grumbling, swearing and complaining, as he met with little or no success. Rarely there would be a chuckle of sheer joy as something succulent went down.

He was deeply engrossed in his task as I padded silently on my way, and the sounds of his feast receded behind me, growing fainter and fainter. I walked for two hours along that line, then turned and retraced my steps. Bruin had gone home by the time I came to the ant hill again, and it was then only half its original height, due to his efforts. I saw nothing else till I reached the Forest Lodge.

Next, I turned up the northern fire-line and walked towards the escarpment. This line did not run straight like the one I had just abandoned. Rather, it twisted and turned considerably as I approached the escarpment. A stream intersected it at the third mile, in which a trickle of clear, cold water sparkled like silver in the moonlight.

Stooping down, I drank, conveying the water to my mouth in my left palm; my right hand held the rifle with its butt to the ground, while my eyes watched the jungle and my ears strained to catch the slightest sound. There was nothing visible, and the only sound was the gurgle of the water. I went on.

The bait I had tied was around the next corner. It was alive, and as I passed it looked at me with dumb reproach for the cruel fate to which I had exposed it. I had no answer, no excuse! That I was guilty there was no doubt. I turned my eyes away, but could not rid myself of the sense of guilt.

At last the base of the escarpment was reached. Here the fire-line stopped and became a narrow game-trail that plunged abruptly into the labyrinth of greenery. It was too dangerous to go any further under such conditions and I turned back.

All I passed on the return journey was a large cobra in the process of swallowing a bamboo-rat. Three-quarters of the rat were down the cobra's throat, only the hindquarters and tail protruding, when I came upon the scene in the middle of the fire-line. The snake saw me and raised its head two feet above the ground, simultaneously erecting the fine bones of its neck to form that most beautiful and at the same time most enthralling of sights' to a newcomer to India; the well-known cobra's hood. The hind legs and tail of the rat still dangled incongruously from its mouth. The beady black eyes glittered malevolently in the phosphorescent light.

I rapidly stamped my feet and clapped my hands. The cobra became nervous and finally panicked. It vomited the rat, lowered itself to the ground with deflated hood, and slithered away into the bushes to one side of the fire-line.

Once more I was back at the bungalow. I had covered twenty miles, and it was 2.45 a.m.

Two fire-lines remained to be tried, but there would only be time to negotiate one, either the fire-line running to the south-east, up which I had not yet been since my arrival, or the line to the south-west, crossing the railway embankment, where I had sat the previous night over the dead body. For some unaccountable reason, I chose the latter.

I reached the railway track, crossed it, and had walked over a mile further towards the west, when suddenly the silence was shattered by the moaning call of a tigress. It appeared to come from a point no more than a couple of furlongs in front of me. Perhaps the beast was walking along the same fire-line; she may have been going away or perhaps coming towards me.

Doubling forward for the next 50 yards, I hid behind the trunk of a large wood-apple tree, cocked the rifle and raised it into position. Then I gave the deep-lunged moan of a male tiger.

Almost immediately it was answered, from much closer than I thought—perhaps a hundred yards away. I did not dare to call again, for fear that I should be recognised for the imposter I was.

Tiger-calling should not be indulged in at close quarters, for fear that the real tiger should discover a difference in the timbre of the call. Should he become suspicious, he may just fade away. One hundred yards is about the closest range at which such mimicry can be tried. Of course, man-eating propensities, and also curiosity, from which most animals suffer to some degree, might still cause the tiger to come forward, but there is always the risk that suspicion may drive him off. So I remained silent—and still.

Thirty seconds later, a tigress strode down the forest-line towards me, the moonlight playing upon the black stripes of her coat. She came abreast of me, then began to pass.

I shot her behind the ear. Only her tail twitched as she sank to the ground. She never knew what happened; she had no chance. It was an unsporting shot.

Anyhow, at Mamandur no human has been killed now for some years. The tigress, which was young, was in the best of condition and there was no reason why she should have become a man-eater. Perhaps, after all, the Chamala man-eater had taught her the bad habit.

Four

The Crossed-Tusker of Gerhetti

THIS IS THE STORY OF ANOTHER ELEPHANT THAT EARNED THE NAME of a 'rogue', and was proscribed by the government of Madras by notification through the Collector and the district Forest Officer of Salem.

The events I am going to relate took place quite a time ago. As usual with rogue elephants, no one knew just what caused this elephant to start molesting human beings. The forest guard then stationed at Gerhetti stated that, one night about a month before the rogue began his depredations, he had heard two bull elephants fighting in the forest. According to his story, the contest had raged off and on for over three hours, and had taken place in the vicinity of a water hole situated just about half a mile in front of the forest bungalow.

Next day he had found the jungle trampled down and great splashes of blood were everywhere in evidence of the punishment that had been inflicted. Judging by the account he gave me, and from the pandemonium that had raged, it must have been a mammoth struggle. Possibly the rogue, as we came to know him, had been the elephant that had got the worst of that fight and from this moment had begun to vent his spleen on all and sundry.

Another explanation might have been that the rogue, was just an ordinary bull elephant in a state of *'musth'* a periodical affliction that affects all elephants and lasts for about three months, during which time they become extraordinarily dangerous.

A third possibility was that this elephant had been wounded by one of the many poachers that are to be found in the forests of Salem district. These gentry sit up over water holes and salt licks to shoot deer that visit such spots during the hot and dry summer months. Generally, when a poacher sees anything more formidable than a harmless deer, he keeps very quiet or slinks away if he feels the going is good. Yet even amongst poachers we find a few that are 'trigger-happy'. They discharge their muskets at any animal that puts in an appearance, and it may have been that one of these adventurers had wounded the bull and started him on his career as a rogue.

It may even have been that a simple peasant, guarding his crops by night, had shot at him with his match-lock. Elephants are fond of destroying crops that grow close to the forest.

Whatever it was that had originally upset him, the rogue of Gerhetti started his career quite suddenly, and for the short time he held sway in the fastness of the jungle where he lived, he became a terror, bringing all traffic, both bullock-cart and pedestrian, to an end within an area of about four hundred square miles.

Gerhetti is the name given to a tiny hamlet comprising some five or six huts about two miles off the track leading from Anchetty to Pennagram in the Salem North Forest Division. The country here is very hilly, and thick bamboo jungle grows to a distance of about three miles from both banks of a rocky stream known as Talvadi Brook, which joins the Cauvery about fifteen miles southwest of the spot I am telling you about. This bamboo jungle nearly always harbours herds of elephant and quite often three or four independent elephants, which although not rogues, are very carefully avoided by the jungle folk.

Another stream, called Gollamothi, flows almost parallel with the Talvadi rivulet, about twelve miles north of it, and joins the Gundalam river, itself another tributary of the Cauvery. These three rivers, with the hills that surround them on all sides, and the thick bamboo jungle that abounds, makes an ideal habitation for any elephant, and it was here that the rogue started his career as a killer.

It began like this. With the midsummer heat, the Gollamothi stream had dried up, except for one or two isolated pools of water which had managed to survive, being formed between huge rocks that cropped up on the riverbed, and fed by subsoil percolation. One of these pools was known to hold fish of some size, perhaps six to eight inches in length, and one afternoon two men from the village of Anchetty, five miles away, decided they would go to this pool and net some fish in the restricted area that had resulted from rapid evaporation.

So they arrived at the pool and cast their nets. Soon they had made a considerable catch. They then put the fish into their baskets and lay down under a shady tree by the side of the water hole to enjoy a brief siesta.

It was about five when one of them awakened. The sun had just sunk behind the top of a hill that jutted out to the west of the pool, but it was still quite bright. As he sat up beside his sleeping companion, something caused the man to look behind him, where he saw the slate-grey bulk of an elephant descending the southern bank of the Gollamothi on its way to the pool.

The man reached out and vigorously shook his companion, to whom he whispered in Tamil '*Anai Varadhu*', which means 'an elephant approaches'. Then he got up and ran to the northern bank and into the forest. His companion, suddenly aroused from sleep, did not quite grasp the significance of the warning, and as he sat looking around and wondering what had happened to his friend, the elephant was upon him.

The man who escaped told me he heard the screams of the friend he had left behind, mingled with the shrill trumpeting of the enraged elephant. Then there was silence. Naturally, he had not waited to hear more. Two days later, when the search party from Anchetty came to look for the remains, they found a pulpy mass of broken flesh and bones decaying in the hot sun. There was evidence that the elephant had first placed his foot upon the man and then had literally torn him apart with his trunk. He had carried one leg to a spot ten yards away, where he had beaten it against the gnarled trunk of a *jumblum* tree before finally throwing it away among the rocks.

That was the rogue's first victim. His second attempt was upon a herd-boy who was driving his herd at sunset to the cattle *patti* at Gundalam. This boy, being young and agile, had fled along the sands of the dry stream, hotly pursued by the vicious elephant. Finding he was losing ground, the boy had the sense to run up the steep side of the hill where the rocks were very slippery and small loose boulders abounded. This had enabled him to maintain his lead.

In his mad rush to escape, the boy cut his bare feet literally to ribbons on the protruding sharp stones, while his body was lacerated in a hundred places by the thorns and shrubs that sought to hold him back. But he had kept on running, and managed to escape the elephant by climbing on to a high rock that protruded about two hundred yards up the hillside.

He told me afterwards that when the bull reached the rock, he walked around it several times, trumpeting and attempting to reach his victim with his trunk. But the boy kept his head, and moved around with the elephant, keeping as far as possible from the tip of that dreaded trunk. He told me that the top of the rock was only about twenty-five square feet in area and that the snake-like tip of the killer's trunk had sometimes been within a foot of his ankles. Nevertheless he had managed to avoid it, and after an hour of this game the elephant suddenly lost interest in his victim and wandered away. Still the boy had been too frightened to come down and had spent the night on top of the rock, only getting down the next morning after the sun had risen high in the heavens, when he felt that the elephant was nowhere in the vicinity.

After this there had been a lull for a month, when the few folk who lived in the area began to feel that the elephant had perhaps departed to other regions, or alternatively, if it had been in *musth*, that *musth* season had elapsed and that its condition had returned to normal.

But they had been far too optimistic, for exactly five weeks after unsuccessfully chasing the herd-boy this elephant attacked two wayfarers as they were journeying through the forest to the village of Nattrapalyam, which lies about eight miles south of Anchetty. These men had been suddenly chased by the rogue and had begun to run along the forest *path* with the animal in hot pursuit about hundred yards behind them. One of these men was about thirty years old and the other some ten years older. Age soon began to tell on the older man causing him to lag behind, his breath coming, in sobbing gasps. He knew that a terrible death was behind him, and he tried his best to keep running. Unfortunately, he had quite lost his head, and made no attempt to circumvent the animal, as he might have done, by perhaps climbing a tree, or by getting behind a rock or even by throwing down a part of his clothing as he ran. This last action might have served to delay the attacker for a few minutes. For when chased by an elephant, it is advisable as a last recourse to shed some part of one's clothing; when the elephant reaches it and catches the strong human smell, he will invariably stop to tear it to ribbons. In the precious seconds thus gained, the victim has a chance of making good his escape.

But this unfortunate man simply ran on till he could run no more. The elephant overtook him as he lay sprawled on the *path*, his body heaving to the gasps of his tortured lungs. Soon their services on this earth were ended, for the elephant picked him up in his trunks and dashed repeatedly against a wayside boulder, beating him to pulp before finally tossing him aside into the jungle.

As a result of these incidents, petitions had been forwarded, through Forest authorities, to the Collector of Salem district to proscribe this animal 'rogue', which means that permission was granted for the elephant to be shot by any game-licence holder in the district. Normally, the elephant is strictly protected in India. Red tapism, as anywhere in the world, is a slow process, and this is particularly the case in India, so that three months or more elapsed before action was taken to issue the necessary order. A further month's delay occurred before all game-licence holders in the district were notified.

Meanwhile the 'rogue' was rather busy. He attacked a bullock-cart that was laden with sandalwood cut by the Forest department. The driver of this cart, and the forest guard who was accompanying the sandalwood, escaped by running into the forest, but the cart was smashed to pieces and one of the bulls slightly injured.

THE CROSSED-TUSKER OF GERHETTI

Not long afterwards, the rogue did rather an unusual thing. Cattle, let loose by graziers in the forest, generally scatter over a fairly wide area. One of these animals evidently strayed too near the rogue, which attacked and broke the beast's back.

A further short lull was followed by the news that he had killed a 'poojaree', one of a jungle tribe of this area, as he was returning with honey from the forest for the contractor who had bought the right from the Forest department to collect all the wild honey in this particular division.

Then the official notification reached me. As a rule, I take no pleasure in elephant-shooting, as I have a very soft corner for these big and noble animals. Secondly, I feel it is a comparatively tame animal itself; elephants invariably give away their position by the noise they make in the undergrowth when feeding. It is then a comparatively simple matter to get up-wind of the quarry and stalk to within a short distance of it. All that is required is a little experience in knowing where to place one's feet, to avoid stepping on dried leaves or twigs that crackle and so give away the stalker's position.

Another very important aspect of 'still hunting' is the ability to 'freeze', to become absolutely still in whatever position you may be at that moment, if the quarry looks your way. This may prove a little awkward at times, when in a half-crouched position, but to straighten up or squat down would be fatal, as the slightest movement involved in doing so will give the stalker away. The thing to do is to remain absolutely and completely 'dead', even for as much as ten minutes in the same half-crouching position. I can assure you that this can sometimes be extremely tiring.

By these methods I have often stalked elephants to within a few yards and watched them grazing peacefully, without their being in the least degree aware of my presence. But the slightest whiff of my scent, or the slightest crackle underfoot, would have sent them thundering away. An elephant has surprisingly poor sight, and if you are dressed in military khaki-green and you keep absolutely still, it will often look your way without ever becoming aware of your presence.

For these reasons, as I have said, I do not like shooting elephants. Also, many of the so-called rogues are not rogues at all. As I have mentioned before, poachers and cultivators are in the habit of firing at elephants and often wound them in the process, when they become embittered against the human race. Again, many of the incidents reported against the so-called rogues never occurred, for people interested in shooting an elephant sometimes concoct tales and urge the villagers to write exaggerated reports in order to induce the Collector to proscribe the rogue. Collectors as a rule go into such matters very carefully and thoroughly before issuing orders; but sometimes, with all these precautions, elephants are killed which are not rogues at all in the real sense.

So I did not pay much heed to the notification till it was followed, about three weeks later, by a letter from Ranga, my *shikari* who lived at the town of Pennagram. He wrote to report that the elephant had killed a poojaree woman four days previously at a spot called Anaibiddamaduvu, which lay about seven miles from Gerhetti. The literal interpretation of this name is 'the pool into which the elephant fell'. It is a natural pool, formed by steep rocks on the bed of Anaibiddahalla river, a sub-tributary of the Chinnar river, which itself is a tributary of the Cauvery, that largest of south Indian rivers. Moreover, this pool is deep and never dries up, and I am told that many years ago an elephant, while reaching for water with its trunk, fell in and could not get out again because of the steep and slippery rocks that ringed it. Elephants are good swimmers, and have herculean strength and endurance, but they also have great bulk; so this poor creature, after swimming round and round in the pool for three days continuously, slowly sank and drowned before quite a large crowd of people who had come all the eleven miles from Pennagram to witness the 'tamasha'.

After receiving Ranga's letter, and as some time had passed since I had last seen him, I got leave of absence for four days and motored down to Pennagram. I picked him up and covered the eighteen miles or more of terribly bad forest road that leads to the Gerhetti forest bungalow, passing Annaibidhamadhuvu on the way.

The forest guard at Gerhetti told me that the rogue was in the vicinity, as well as a herd of about ten elephants. All these animals were in the habit of drinking at the water hole in front of the bungalow, and as there were several animals in the herd of about the same size as the rogue, it would be difficult to know which was which. This precluded any possibility of following with any degree of certainty any particular set of tracks.

Further, the description of this animal in the notification was very vague; it merely stated that the measurement around the circumference of the forefoot had been 4'10", which made the elephant approximately 9'.8" tall, as twice the circumference of the forefoot is the approximate height. The colour was reported as black, but all elephants are black after they have washed, but they soon cover themselves with sand or earth. Sand in the forest is of different hues, varying from red to brown, grey, and almost black. So this was no distinguishing factor either. The only feature that appeared to identify the elephant was that the two tusks, which were reported to be over three feet long, met and crossed near their tips.

You will therefore understand that the last factor was the only one by which I would be able to identify this particular animal, for it was doubtful if he would give permission, to approach and measure his height! But to see if the tusks were crossed meant getting a frontal or head-on view of the elephant, as at an angle tusks may appear to cross without actually doing so. I certainly did not want to shoot the wrong animal, apart from the immense amount of trouble and official explanation that would follow.

This meant that I could select any set of tracks that came up to the measurement of the rogue and follow them till I came upon the animal that had made them, then manoeuvre for a frontal view of the animal to see whether he possessed the hallmark of crossed-tusks. If he did, he was my elephant. If he did not, I would have to start all over again by going back to the pool and following another set of tracks. It must be remembered that I had only four days at my disposal, and of these four days one had already passed in picking up Ranga, coming to Gerhetti and making the necessary inquiries.

At about ten that night I heard the sound of elephants feeding in the vicinity of the pool. This was undoubtedly the herd, and the rogue would not be with them. So I went to sleep again.

At dawn I started with Ranga and the forest guard on my plan of following up one of the sets of tracks. The margin of the water hole was fairly ploughed up by a mass of footprints of all sizes, where the herd had watered the night before. These included the tracks of some very young elephants, which could hardly have been over three feet tall.

Circumventing the pool, I found three sets of tracks which came near to the size of the rogue. Two of these three sets, I noticed, had been made on the same side of the pool as the herd had watered, while the remaining set had been made by an elephant which had approached the water from quite another direction. I therefore argued that this third animal might be the rogue, and we began to track him in single file. Ranga went in front, following the tracks; I followed, covering him with my double-barrelled 450/400 Jeffries; the Forest Guard came behind me, his duty being to guard against an attack from the rear in case it happened that the elephant had gone round in a semicircle, and was now grazing behind us.

For a short distance after leaving the water the ground was covered by long spear grass and clearly revealed the passage of the elephant the night before, being trampled flat in all directions. Then the spear grass gave way to the usual thorny growth of lantana and wait-a-bit thorn. Here also it was comparatively easy to see where our quarry had passed, but our own passage became more difficult by reason of the thorns that plucked and tore at our clothing.

Yet the tracks were clear and we made fairly good time for about a mile, when we reached the base of a small hill. The slopes of this hill were covered with heavy bamboo growth, and the elephant had passed through this, climbing the hill as he went. He had also stopped to feed on the tender shoots that spring from the end of the fronds of bamboo, as was clearly evident by the havoc he had created in the mass of broken bamboo stems we met along this trail. Here he had passed a considerable quantity of dung, and as we reached the top of the hill and went down the other side, it was evident that the elephant had fed until the early hours of that morning; for the dung was fresh and had not had time to cool.

From here onwards our passage became laboriously slow. The dense bamboo completely surrounded us and a careless step by any one of us resulted in a rustle or sharp crackle, depending on whether we trod upon the leaves or bamboo fronds.

I touched Ranga's elbow and motioned to him to stand still, the guard and myself doing the same. We listened for over ten minutes for the familiar sounds of a feeding elephant, or the deep rumble that issues from his cavernous stomach in the process of digestion. But the forest was comparatively silent except for the cheery calls of grey junglecocks everywhere around us, and the distant whoops of langur monkeys on the opposite hillside.

Evidently our quarry was resting, or had perhaps passed further down into the deep valley that lay before us. As the latter seemed more likely, we proceeded on tiptoe, slowly and carefully in his wake. We had all to keep our eyes down to make sure we did not trample on anything that would betray our presence. Another half mile brought us to the valley, where the undergrowth was extremely dense; wild plum, wood-apple, and mighty tamarind trees grew profusely everywhere, making visibility beyond fifteen to twenty yards impossible. Another two hundred yards brought us to the rocky bed of a small tributary of the Gollamothi river.

The elephant had here skirted the bed of the stream and crossed it at a sandy spot fifty yards further down. The opposite bank, up which he had then climbed, was fairly steep, so that we were now faced with the prospect of having the elephant above us, which is hardly the best way of meeting a 'rogue'.

We went forward very slowly indeed, and as silently as was humanly possible. Our quarry had stopped feeding, and was now on the move again. We soon saw that he appeared to be making for another valley that lay beyond the spur of the hill up which we were now climbing. Having reached this conclusion, we began to move faster, but had gone only another quarter-mile when we heard the rumbling sound made by the elephant's stomach in the process of digesting his heavy meal.

THE CROSSED-TUSKER OF GERHETTI

I sent Ranga and the forest guard up a stout tamarind tree and crept forward alone in the direction of the sound. The elephant was in a small depression, densely wooded by bamboo. Evidently he was resting, or perhaps lying down, as there were no sounds of his feeding. By this time the rumbling had also ceased.

Very carefully, almost inch by inch, I went down into the depression. Then stopping for a moment, I gathered a little soft earth in my hand and held it up before me, letting it drop in order to see from which direction any current of air might be blowing. The earth fell straight, indicating that there was hardly any breeze in the depression. This was a handicap, as there was a chance of the elephant smelling me in the still air.

So I went forward, still more carefully, if that were possible. The bamboos towered above me, and I peeped around each clump as I came abreast of it. A few more yards of this sort of progress and I saw what appeared to be a slate-grey boulder before me. It was the elephant, lying on the ground, and as my bad luck would have it, facing in the opposite direction.

I could now do one of two things: either make a detour and try to come upon the elephant from the front, where I might see his tusks and identify him as the rogue before shooting, or much simpler, rouse him from where I stood. He would undoubtedly turn around to face the disturbance, so that I could then identify him and shoot before he could know what was happening.

Deciding on this second and easier course, I slipped partly behind a clump of bamboo, then softly whistled. The elephant took no notice. Perhaps he was deeply asleep, or thought the sound had come from some forest bird. Then I clicked my tongue loudly. This had the desired effect, for the elephant scrambled to its feet and span around to face me.

He was a magnificent tusker, quite ten feet tall, and his ivory tusks gleamed magnificently in the early morning sunlight. But they were wide apart, not crossed in the least. I had spent my time tracking the wrong elephant.

The pachyderm looked at me in amazement for quite half a minute, his small eyes contemplating the creature who had disturbed his slumber. I could almost read the thoughts that were passing through his brain. His first reaction, after surprise, was annoyance and he moved forward a pace or two in a threatening attitude. I gave another sharp whistle, at the sound of which his courage ebbed away, and he turned tail and bolted into the forest, the crashing sound of his retreat dying away in the distance.

By the time I returned to the spot where I had left Ranga and the Forest Guard, they had already climbed down from the tamarind tree, guessing, by the sounds they had clearly heard, that I had found an animal which was not the rogue we were after. The three of us then trudged dejectedly back to the water hole, not only disappointed, but annoyed at the time we had wasted.

As previously related, there were two other tracks of approximately the same size. They had been made in the mud of the pool and nothing could be gained by measuring them with my tape to determine which came nearest to the notified dimensions of the rogue; soft mud exaggerated the track of any animal. Ranga followed one, and the guard and myself the other, with the understanding that we would return to the water hole in fifteen minutes for further consultation.

It was not long before I could see that the animal I was following had been one of the regular herd, for the broken undergrowth revealed the presence of the feeding cows and young that had accompanied him. He was obviously not the rogue, and in exactly fifteen minutes by my watch I turned and made my way back to the water hole. Ranga, having no watch, had not yet arrived, so I sat down to a quiet pipe and sip of hot tea from the flask carried by the Forest Guard. After about ten minutes, he came to report that the elephant had made a detour a quarter of a mile from the water hole, had moved around in a semicircle and passed through a strip of jungle that led to a hill in exactly the opposite direction, behind the bungalow.

This news seemed promising, so we were up and away. Nor was it long before we came to the spot whence Ranga had returned to report. It soon became evident that our new quarry was a traveller, for he had hardly stopped to feed, other than pluck an occasional small stem of succulent young leaves. That elephant led us on and on, over the hill behind the forest bungalow, over the next two hills, and then in almost a straight line to the Talvadi stream.

In all we covered well over four miles before reaching the bed of that stream, when we found that the elephant had turned southwest and was moving directly down the Talvadi river itself. I knew the Cauvery river lay within a distance of fifteen miles, and I began to feel our quarry had suddenly made up his mind to reach the big river. Once he did this, and particularly if he swam across to the opposite bank, it would be hopeless to follow him, as the terrain there is not only extremely dense, but leads on and on as unbroken forest and hill country to the Niligiri and Biligirirangan Mountains, over a hundred miles away.

So we passed on with all possible speed, casting discretion to the winds, but our elephant had had a lead of several hours, and judging by the long and determined strides he had taken, he had been bent upon travelling.

The soft sand of the riverbed was now scalding hot under the midday sun. It hampered my walking and trickled into my boots by means that only fine river or sea sand knows. Every now and again the streambed became rocky, and for long stretches the fine sand gave way to a succession of rounded, water-worn boulders. In such spots the elephant had pushed through the undergrowth of the banks to avoid the boulders, and we did the same, bent double to dodge the dangling lines of creepers, and pouring with perspiration from our exertions.

Fifteen miles of such walking brought us near the confluence of Talvadi and the Cauvery. A few hundred yards from the big river, the Talvadi stream is crossed by the rough track leading from Uttaimalai village to Biligundlu. The elephant had changed direction here and had followed the track towards Uttaimalai for another two miles, before turning southwards again towards a swamp that borders the big river. This swamp, known as Kartei Palam, which means Bison Hollow, was well known to me. Years before it had been a regular haunt for bison herds that swam across the Cauvery from the Coimbatore bank to the Salem side. At this time of the year the swamp was fairly dry except in places, but lush grass grew everywhere, while shady clumps of trees dotted the whole area.

We now met with signs that the elephant had begun feeding, and as we made our way towards the centre of the swamp mounds of fresh dung showed that the animal was not far away.

The ground also became boggy, and once more I sent Ranga and the guard back to minimise the squelching sounds that were bound to arise from three people walking in the mud. Progress was necessarily at a snail's pace, for I had not only to look out for the elephant, but study the ground carefully at each step, to avoid suddenly plunging waist-deep into the clinging black clay. Yet, several times I sank knee-deep, and to extricate myself I had to struggle and flounder about, making no end of noise, before I gained a firmer footing.

Several times I stopped to listen but heard nothing, and then, without warning, there came a violent 'swoosh' of the reedy grass, and the elephant stood some twenty paces away, all dripping and covered with the sticky muck in which he had been lying. It was a big bull, with gleaming white tusks, symmetrically curved. But they were not the crossed tusks of the rogue. Disappointment and disgust so overcame me that I fairly 'shoo-ed' that poor elephant away, and when I rejoined my followers, I was in no good mood, as they could clearly see.

It was now past 4 p.m., and we had some fifteen miles to retrace along the Talvadi Stream, plus another four to the Gerhetti bungalow. Alternatively, we could camp at Biligundlu and return next morning; but this would mean the loss of another half-day, out of the two days that were left to me. So I gave the order for the return march, much to the disgust of my companions, who reminded me that, as we had no light of any kind, the major portion of our journey would have to be performed in darkness, there being no moon. We might even meet the elephant! My reply, I am afraid, was terse, and consigned this elephant, and all other elephants, to a region they would find far too hot.

That return journey seemed one long succession of stumbling, slipping, slithering over rocks, or tripping over stumps, or being caught by creepers without sign or sound of the elephant. It was almost midnight before we limped into the Gerhetti bungalow, thoroughly exhausted and as fretful as children. We had been up with the dawn, walking incessantly, stalking through thorns, grass, river-sand and swamp, and had covered about forty miles. We were ravenously hungry and thirsty too.

Next morning I was cramped and footsore. The forest guard showed an ankle, which he had contrived to twist somewhere along the Talvadi stream, and begged to be excused from that day's operations. Only Ranga appeared fit, and ready for another hard day. Porridge, bacon and eggs, and strong coffee put new life into me, while a huge ball of *'ragi'*, which is a small foodgrain, boiled and made into a sphere almost the size of a tiny cannonball, washed down with coffee, would satisfy Ranga till nightfall.

We had all been too tired to hear any sounds during the night, but a visit to the water hole now indicated the herd had returned while we had slept. There were also the fresh footmarks of two big bulls, one of which was probably the first elephant I had followed the previous day, while the other was the animal I had not followed at all. The third bull, as we well knew, we had left far away at Kartei Palam.

Nevertheless, nothing could be left to chance; so we followed the same plan as that of the previous day, tracking each of these two animals till we came up with them. By 9.30 a.m. we had come up to the first bull that we had decided to follow. He was slightly smaller than the two we had tracked the previous day, and he was not the rogue! No doubt this was the third animal of the trio whose footprints we had noted the previous day. Going back to the water hole, we set out on the remaining track, and came upon its maker at 2.30 p.m., quietly standing under a large and shady tamarind tree. Nor was he the rogue. I readily recognised him as the first animal I had tracked the previous day and had disturbed while lying among the bamboos.

Thus it was clear that the 'rogue' was not in the immediate vicinity. Three of the four days available to me had now gone, but I was still no further forward than on the day of my arrival.

THE CROSSED-TUSKER OF GERHETTI

At five we were back at the bungalow, brewing a large *degchie* of tea. Then at half-past five a party of bullock-carts arrived from Anchetty, eight miles away, to shelter for the night because of the presence of the rogue. The cartmen stated that at a spot about half-way from Anchetty, where the Gollamothi stream traversed the road, they had come upon the tracks of a large elephant which had crossed and recrossed the road at several points and was evidently hanging around not far from the ford itself.

Determined not to give up till the last moment, Ranga and I ate an early dinner and, bundling the still-tired Forest Guard into the car, motored to the ford of which the cartmen had spoken.

It was 7 p.m. when we arrived there and almost dark. The car lights revealed the tracks of the elephant where the cartmen had said. At the ford itself, with the aid of torches we made out the plate-like spoor of the elephant superimposed upon the narrow ruts made by the cartwheels of our friends. Elephants do not wander about in daytime in hot weather, and this clearly indicated that the pachyderm had been on the road that very evening, before our arrival. Perhaps he had even heard the sound of the car, or seen our lights, and had moved off just before we came on the scene.

We quickly lowered the hood of the Studebaker. I handed my 'sealed-beam' spotlight to Ranga, whom I placed in the 'dickie' seat behind, but kept the guard in the front seat. I myself sat on the folded hood, my feet on the driving seat, with my rifle and torch at the ready. Complete darkness soon enveloped us, overshadowed as we were by the towering *muthee* and *jumlum* trees that bordered the banks of the Gollamothi, together with bamboo clumps, whose stems creaked weirdly to the jungle air-currents that blew up and down the dry sandy bed of the river.

The prospects were poor. To begin with, we did not know whether the tracks we had seen belonged to the rogue. They might, indeed, have been made by any elephant. All we knew for certain was that they had not been made by any of the three big males around Gerhetti. Secondly, there was not the slightest reason for this elephant to return to the ford he had so recently passed, for he had the whole wide jungle in which to roam. Thirdly, we all knew that ten miles to an elephant is scarcely two hours' easy ambling, and that when he is really travelling he moves much faster. Fourthly, the wind was blowing in all directions, and would carry our scent to any elephant within a quarter-of-a-mile and, if he was not the rogue, drive him off. On the other hand, there was the slender hope that, if this was the rogue, our scent might attract him.

So we waited in the pitch-darkness till 8.30 p.m., and then the dull sound of a hollow log being turned over came to us form somewhere upstream. The elephant was on the move at last and, judging by the sound, was some four or five hundred yards away. Silence followed for another quarter-hour, when the sharp crack of a breaking branch, much closer, indicated that the elephant was feeding and moving towards the ford as he did so.

I knew he would take thirty minutes at least to finish eating the young leaves from the ends of the branch he had just broken, so that there would be plenty of time before he came near. The car, with us inside it, would be clearly visible to him as he came around the curve of the river, and there was every possibility, if he was not the rogue, that on seeing us he would just fade quietly away into the forest. But I had not taken the wind into consideration; just then it blew strongly from us towards the elephant.

Minuets of silence followed, and then we heard a slight rustling in the undergrowth from the bank of the river nearest

THE CROSSED-TUSKER OF GERHETTI

to the car. It was a faint sound, apparently made by a small body in the bushes. Then the ominous crack of trodden bamboo came to us suddenly. Silence again, deep and enveloping. Even the breeze seemed to have died, to allow full opportunity for the next event.

This was the ear-splitting scream of a charging bull-elephant, mingled with the crashing of bamboos and undergrowth as they collapsed before the monster that rushed towards us.

Ranga never flinched! The beam of the spot-light cut through the enveloping gloom. My own torch-beam, mingling with that of the vastly more brilliant spotlight, showed an enormous tusker, his bulk pitch black, his trunk curled upwards and inwards, with two wicked white tusks that were crossed at the tip, thundering upon us!

At fifty yards range the bullet from my right barrel took him in the throat. He stopped with the impact, screaming with rage. No doubt this was more than he had bargained for! The explosion, the pain and the lights confused him, and he half-turned into the jungle. My second bullet, aimed hastily at the temple, struck him somewhere on the side of the head. He rushed into the jungle, stumbled on his forefeet, picked himself up again as I reloaded, and disappeared in the bamboos as my third shot struck him somewhere in the body. For quite fifteen minutes we could hear heavy crashes in the jungle as the elephant reeled, collapsed and then recovered, to continue his flight.

Starting the car, I reversed and returned to Gerhetti. I slept soundly that night, Ranga awakening me at dawn with a mugful of steaming, strong tea.

By 6.30 a.m., we were on the track of the stricken rogue. Great gouts of blood had issued from the throat-wound and had sprayed through his trunk over the surrounding bushes, which had been reddened by his passage. Soon we too were red with his blood as we pushed ourselves through the undergrowth in his wake.

He had lain, or fallen down, in several places, where the greensward had been dyed a deep red. He had leaned against several tree-trunks that were still sticky with his blood. Truly, if you do not finish the job of killing an elephant, you let yourself in for a gory trail. I really pitied this poor beast, murderous killer of men though he had been.

After two miles I found him, half-kneeling, half-lying against a tree-trunk. He was so weak from loss of blood that he could scarcely move, although he clearly saw me as I walked towards him. The only sign of life were his wicked little blood-shot eyes, that gleamed and moved as they watched my approach. Fifteen yards away I raised my rifle to deliver the coup de grace. As if to salute approaching death, that game and mighty beast shivered from head to foot as he drew up his mighty bulk to its full ten feet. The trunk curled upwards, the big ears flapped outward, and he staggered two paces forward in his last charge, when the heavy 450/400 bullet crashed into his temple and he collapsed, as if pole-axed, to earth.

Although a killer, the 'crossed-tusker of Gerhetti' was a brave fighter, and I honoured him as he lay before my still-smoking muzzle—mighty in life and even mightier in his death!

Five

The Sangam Panther

NEWS FILTERED THROUGH TO MY HOME IN BANGALORE THAT A leopard, or 'panther' as it is more commonly known in India, was killing people in the vicinity of a place called Sangam, a little over seventy miles south of the city.

Man-eating panthers are rare in southern India. To begin with, the jungles are not so extensive, or nearly so continuously mountainous as in the north, particularly along the foothills of the vast Himalayan range. The exception is the Western Ghats, which are almost wholly covered with forest for over four hundred miles, with an average breadth of ten to fifteen miles. But the other forest areas are of much smaller extent and are more or less surrounded by cultivation. This causes carnivores, and particularly panthers, to confine their attentions to the herds of cattle and goats, in which the country is abundantly rich, and to a lesser extent to village curs, locally known as *'piedogs'* which are, like the common monkey, the curse of the land. Prior to the advent to hydrophobia vaccine, large numbers of persons died yearly of infection from the bite of mad dogs, as these curs constantly contract rabies, especially in the hot weather. Monkeys are and always have been a major menace, doing untold damage to crops and fruit trees. The monkey has a strong religious significance to Indians, and great objection is raised against any attempt to harm it. Panthers—at least so far as the *'piedogs'* and monkeys are concerned—therefore perform a great service to the land.

In the Western Ghats of which I have just spoken, the rainfall is very heavy, even exceeding hundred inches per year. They are covered with dense bamboo, long grass, and thick evergreen vegetation—the breeding grounds of clouds of mosquitoes, ticks, leeches, flies and other animal pests.

Panthers do not like much water—and they detest the pests, in any and all their many forms! So, in the only region where they could multiply unmolested they are hardly to be found! By a natural arrangement, therefore, panthers, which are found in all other jungles of southern India, generally have plenty to eat and somehow do not become addicted to the bad habit of man-eating. A notable exception to this was the panther of Gummalapur, a story I have related elsewhere*; in that case there were special circumstances that caused it to take to man-eating.

In Bangalore news often reached us of people being mauled by panthers and tigers, more often by the former. But nobody took particular notice of these rumours as on-the-spot investigation always told the same tale. Some villager, with his matchlock, or some inexperienced hunter would let fly at a panther, generally with slugs, and succeed only in hurting

---

* In *Nine Man-Eaters and One Rogue,* George Allen and Unwin, 1954.

THE SANGAM PANTHER

it. Then, inexperienced in jungle-lore, he would attempt to follow it up, through lantana bushes or amongst rocks, and get mauled—sometimes severely—for his pains. In years gone by, over seventy-five per cent of such cases of mauling resulted in death from septicaemia. With the advent of the sulpha drugs, casualties dropped to below ten per cent.

So nobody took much notice when such news came in. Why should they? They had other work to do. Moreover, rumour is invariably much exaggerated in India! A slight scratch is magnified into a severed mauling, and a mauling into a killing. When an actual killing does occur, it is widely described in the Press as several killings.

Therefore, when I heard that a panther had killed a woman, and later killed and eaten a child at Sangam, I did not believe it. Then the panther killed a third and a fourth time. The Press got hold of the news and it was splashed across the front pages.

Several hunters from Bangalore, Mysore and Madras went after the animal, but for a month the panther did not kill. One of the hunters succeeded in shooting a panther; and this fact, coupled with the cessation of human kills, seemed to indicate that it was the man-eater that had been shot. The hunters returned to the towns.

Then the panther killed once more, but was prevented from eating its victim, a man who was sleeping in a shed-like room with a pack of four mongrel dogs, with which he used to hunt hare and sometimes deer.

A thorn fence protected the entrance to the shed. The roof comprised loose bits of zinc sheeting, and the wall consisted of wooden stakes driven into the ground in close formation, the gaps being stuffed with thorns. The panther came at night, and with its paws contrived to open a passage between the end stake of the doorway and the thorn fence across the entrance. The dogs panicked, barking and howling loudly and cowering to one side. But the man must have just woken.

The panther entered the shed. The dogs clustered together but did nothing, and the marauder, walking past them, grabbed the man by the throat. He died after uttering a single, piercing wail.

The people in the neighbouring hut had been disturbed by the noise made by the dogs' barking and growling in the shed. They wondered what was happening, but nobody would go outside to investigate. The panther then tried to drag the dead man out of the shed through the same gap by which it had entered. The gap was not big enough. So the panther itself passed through and tried to drag the man after it. But the body became entangled in the thorns and stuck fast. The panther then gave a mighty heave, which succeeded in unbalancing the fence, which fell with a crash on top of the animal. This must have frightened him considerably for he made off, leaving the corpse still entangled amongst the thorns.

The continued noise resulting from the efforts of the panther now alarmed the people in the next hut, who had been listening breathlessly all this time. They began to shout and woke other villagers. After quite a while, some of the brave men came forth carrying lanterns, armed with matchlocks, bludgeons and staves, to find the dead man, but no panther.

The alarm now spread afresh, and news was brought to me by the village *Patel*, or headman, who came to Bangalore expressly for the purpose. I was at that time able to take two days' casual leave, while Sunday made a third. So I agreed to go with him and attempt to shoot the panther within those three days.

The road to Sangam ran past the town of Kankanhalli, thirty-six miles from Bangalore, from where it began to descend

THE SANGAM PANTHER

sharply to the bed of the Cauvery river. The last ten miles of the track was really atrocious, and my Studebaker rocked and creaked and groaned in all its joints, in protest at such bad treatment. Hairpin bends at ridiculous gradients and sharp angles (where all milestones and furlong slabs were coloured black to prevent them from being uprooted by wild elephants, who have a great aversion to anything white), betokened my approach to journey's end, and soon I reached the little traveller's bungalow after a short but exceedingly tough journey.

The word 'Sangam' denotes a 'joining' or 'confluence', and was most appropriate, for it marked the junction of the Cauvery river with its tributary, the Arkravarthy, which flows in almost a straight line southwards from its source north of Bangalore.

The Cauvery here flows from west to east, Sangam being on its northern bank within Mysore state territory. The southern bank of the Cauvery comes within the jungles of North Coimbatore district (Kollegal Forest Division). Some thirteen miles east of Sangam, Mysore state territory ends and is flanked by Salem district, which thereafter holds the northern bank of the river with North Coimbatore district continuing along the southern bank. Both North Coimbatore and Salem districts belong to the Madras presidency.

Sangam is a beautifully wooded spot, offering in normal times first-rate masher fishing, with crocodile shooting among the sandbanks and rocks in any direction along the river. On the Mysore side of the forest there are spotted deer, sambar, barking-deer, wild pig, feathered game, and an occasional bear, panther or tiger. Elephants often cross over from the Coimbatore bank. Along the southern bank, in the Coimbatore jungles, all the above abound in greater number, in addition to several fine herds of bison. Elephant and bear are particularly numerous.

After parking the car under the huge *muthee* trees that flanked the river and grew beside the bungalow, I walked across to the small village where the dog-keeper had recently been killed and inspected the scene for myself, in addition to being given graphic accounts of what had happened by the neighbours, who had heard so much that day, but had done nothing to help the poor fellow. The *Patel*, who had returned with me joined in the voluble tale.

With much questioning and cross-questioning, it became apparent that this panther was going to be an exceedingly difficult animal to bag, as on the north banks of the river it had a very wide expanse of jungle to wander over, without taking into consideration the many square miles of forest on the southern or Coimbatore side. But the latter could reasonably be excluded, since panthers, unlike tigers, generally dislike swimming across big rivers, although they swim well when compelled to do so.

The first, and apparently only thing to do was to tie out baits. With the *Patel's* active help, I purchased five large bull-calves. The first of these we tethered about half-a-mile west of the bungalow and about the same distance from the river bank; the second, on a line roughly parallel with the river and a mile farther west; the third, a mile farther west than the second; the fourth, on the farther bank of the Arkravarthy tributary, about half-a-mile east of the bungalow and the same distance from the Cauvery; and the fifth, a mile east of the fourth bait. Thus the five baits were roughly in a straight line, flanking the river, about half-a-mile inland and with a distance of four miles between the farthest bait to the west and the farthest bait to the east.

It was sunset before I returned to the bungalow. A cold dinner appeased my appetite, eaten on the small bungalow verandah and washed down with two steaming mugs of tea.

THE SANGAM PANTHER

After lighting my pipe, I sat with my back to the wall, listening to the subdued rush of the river as it sped along its rocky bed. It was a dark night and fairly cloudy. Such stars as could be seen peeping occasionally between clouds would be insufficient for night-watching, so I went inside and fell asleep.

Early next morning we checked the baits. They were all alive. I walked up the road down which I had come the previous day, climbing up the hairpin bends and ghat section. There were no panther tracks to bee seen. A herd of spotted deer and three sambar—singly and at different places—had crossed the road during the night, but no other animal had passed.

When returning to the bungalow, instead of coming back along the road, I cut down the hill through the jungle and came on to the dry bed of the Arkravarthy, where I turned southwards and walked in the sand, looking for possible pugmarks. There were none to be seen, but the same herd of spotted deer that had crossed the road had also traversed the sands. In due course, I passed my bait number four, and came to where the Arkravarthy joined the Cauvery.

A day and a half, out of the three days at my disposal, had now passed, and I had not even seen the panther's pugmarks. The situation seemed hopeless.

After lunch, I decided to walk in the easterly direction, downstream along the Cauvery for about three-and-a-half miles, to a gorge where the river narrowed to about twenty feet. At this spot it roared through a chasm, known as Meke-Dat. The meaning of that word, in Kanarese language, is 'the goat's leap'. Legend records that, years and years ago, a jungle-sheep pursued by wild dogs on the Coimbatore side and driven to the brink of the river, performed the prodigious feat of leaping those twenty feet to safety on the Mysore side.

Here, all other sounds are drowned by the roar of the turbulent waters, hurling themselves through the narrow opening, and a man can hardly hear himself even when he shouts his very loudest.

I sat on the edge of the rocks and watched the troubled, racing river. A hundred yards away, downstream where the surface had become placid again, an occasional fish broke water, leaping into the air, as if evincing sheer exuberance and joy of living. A fish-eagle circled in the ethereal blue of a clear sky. After a while, I rose and retraced my steps to the bungalow. I had still not found any panther tracks.

The night was clear. Although there was no moon, there were none of the previous night's clouds and the starlight was enough in the jungle to enable one to see for a few yards.

The watchman in charge of the bungalow owned a *'piedog'*—the name by which mongrels in India are known—and against my custom and only because time was so short, I asked him to lend it to me till midnight. He hummed and hawed at first, but when three rupees had changed hands he agreed.

While walking along the road that day, I had noticed a rock at its edge hardly a mile away. I took the dog, tied it at the foot of the rock and walked away down the road. When out of sight of the dog, I turned to my right and cut into the jungle, coming back to the rock on its 'off' side. Silently I clambered up, and lay flat on its top. The rock was still warm from the sun that had been shining on it all day.

Thinking it had been abandoned, the dog began barking, whining and howling by turns. Dogs are too intelligent, it is unfair to tie them out as bait. Unlike cattle and goats, they sense danger at once and, even if not attacked, go through hours of mental agony. I have known a dog which was tied out as bait for a panther—although it was not harmed—

THE SANGAM PANTHER

become so nervous that it fell sick the following day and died within a week.

I watched from the top of the rock. Nearly an hour passed, and then suddenly a shadowy, grey shape came scampering down the road. It moved fast till about ten feet from the dog, then it stopped. Could it be the panther? The stars shed just enough light to prevent the darkness from being total, but not more than that. I could just see the grey shape looking at the dog. The dog growled furiously as it turned round to face the intruder. It must be a panther, I thought, as I aligned my rifle in its direction preparatory to depressing the switch of my torch which was fastened along the barrel.

'Ha! Ha! Ha! Ha! Ha!' said the intruder, followed by a disparaging but loud 'Cheey! Shee-ay! Shee-ay!'

It was a hyaena, the common striped hyaena of southern India. The dog growled still more ferociously; then began to bark frenziedly..

Now began an amusing drama, such as watchers by night are sometimes privileged to witness in a jungle. The hyaena darted off the road into the undergrowth, where he began to say, 'Gudda! Guddar! Garrar! Gurr-rr-aa!' ending with his usual disparaging 'Cheey-ar! Shee-ar!'

The dog faced the noise and barked loudly. The hyaena reappeared on the road, beyond the dog but watching him, and crackled, 'Ha! Ha! ha! Guddar! Garrar! Shee-ay!'

Unlike his African cousins, the spotted and the brown hyaena, the former being the familiar 'laughing hyaena' we have all heard about, the Indian hyaena is generally a silent animal, hunting alone or at the most in pairs. Spotted hyaenas move in packs. As a rule, all hyaenas are cowardly animals, although they are extremely strong for their size and have enormously powerful jaws, which can easily bite right through a man's arm, bone and all.

Quite rarely, they display extraordinary courage, of which I once saw an example. I had been sitting over a panther kill. The owner turned up and began to eat. I had held my shot, as I wanted, if possible, to learn the sex of the animal before killing it. This was because I had been told a male and a female panther lived in the vicinity, and that the female was accompanied by two cubs about six months old. I wanted to make certain I did not shoot the mother.

While I hesitated, a hyaena had arrived on the scene, and his arrival, on that occasion, had been dramatic. He came as if from nowhere, and the first I knew of his arrival was when he had scampered boldly up to the panther, voicing the same medley of sounds I have just described. The panther, sprawled across its kill, had glared at the newcomer with blazing orbs, snarling and growling furiously. The hyaena had approached to within five feet, just beyond reach of the panther's paw-sweep, and had set up such a cacophony of hideous sound as to resemble a chorus of the demons of hell.

The panther had added to the noise by growling still louder, and every now and then striking at the hyaena with its claws. The latter just rocked backwards, out of reach of each blow, after which it would feint with a short rush forward, while gradually working around to the rear of the panther. At first the panther had turned around correspondingly, to keep the hyaena in view, growling even more loudly while making short jabs and slaps with its paws in the direction of the hyaena. But the hyaena, always out of reach, had haw-ed and sneered, gargled and gurgled with unabated zeal.

Frightened—or perhaps just disgusted—at the unseemly racket, the panther had finally risen from its kill and then walked slowly away with many a backward glance, amidst snarls, at the hyaena, who continued his weird din till the panther had vanished in the undergrowth. Then he had fallen upon the kill himself, with the greatest—and, no doubt, thoroughly deserved—enthusiasm.

But the hyaena which I continued to watch from the rock was undoubtedly a little scared of the mongrel dog. Frequently he would disappear to one or the other side of the road. Then would come a pitter-patter amongst the dried leaves as he doubled back and forth, this way and that, to reappear at all places while continuing to make his unseemly, weird and often comical sounds.

The lesson I learnt from these two experiences was that hyaenas try to frighten their opponents with their continuous, unseemly crackle. The first hyaena had frightened the panther off its own kill while this one was trying to frighten the dog, perhaps just to clear it off the road or into the undergrowth, where he could pounce upon it more easily.

But the dog was tied up, and so could not move away, which the hyaena could not understand. An hour of this sort of thing ceased to be amusing to me, and I realised the racket, especially the part played by the hyaena, was almost certain to drive away any panther in the vicinity, man-eater or otherwise. So, groping for a small piece of rock, I hurled it at the hyaena. My aim fell short of its mark, and the stone thudded on the hard surface of the road. The hyaena jumped nervously, and scampered into the bushes, while the dog stopped barking and began to whimper. I thought I had rid the scene of a most unwelcome visitor.

Perhaps a quarter of an hour had passed when I heard the furtive pitter-patter again, shortly followed by the hyaena's queer notes. The dog barked and growled. I threw another stone at the hyaena. He stopped; only to start again after ten minutes. Once more a stone; once more a silence, followed by a new beginning. Only after about the fifth stone did the hyaena feel that the spot had somehow become unhealthy, and with a final, 'Ah! Ah! Ah! Chee-ey! Shee-ay!' took himself off. It was past ten o'clock.

My watch showed five minutes to midnight when I heard the approach of human voices. A little later, I saw the twinkling lights of two lanterns, illuminating from that distance the walking feet of many men. The dog saw them and stopped its moaning.

When the party drew level with the dog, I counted eleven men, two of whom were carrying lanterns, and all of whom, except one, carried staves and lathis of some sort or another.

The one exception was armed with a matchlock. They had obviously come in search of me. I answered their call and came down from the rock.

The men then told me that, scarcely an hour earlier, the panther had made its way into one of the huts of the very village where the dog-keeper had been attacked by burrowing through the thatched wall, and had seized one of the five sleeping inmates, a woman about twenty-five years old. She had shrieked aloud as she found herself being dragged away, waking the other four persons in the room, who were her father, two brothers and mother.

Meanwhile, the panther was trying to drag her out through the opening in the thatch by which it had entered. The girl struggled violently. The panther dropped her and bit her viciously. One of the brothers struck a match to lighten the darkness of the hut's interior. Her father, with commendable bravery and presence of mind, hurled the only missile which came to his hand, at the panther. The missile happened to be a brass water-pot of some weight, and it struck the panther full on its side. Man-eaters, whether tigers or panthers, invariably have a streak of cowardice in their natures and this panther was no exception to the general rule. Leaving its victim, it had dashed out of the hut through the opening in the thatch.

The screams of the mauled woman and the general pandemonium had awakened the whole village. The menfolk came out with lanterns, armed as best as they could. The party of eleven had then come to the rest-house to find me, and the watchman from whom I had borrowed the dog had directed them to where I was sitting.

Telling one of the men to untie the rope and bring the dog in tow, we hastened back to the bungalow, and I brought out my first-aid kit from the back seat of the Studebaker. We then hurried on to the village, where an appalling sight awaited me. The poor girl had been bitten right through her right shoulder, and again in the abdomen, where the panther had seized her the second time when she had struggled to escape. One breast and her chest right down the side were in ribbons where the foul claws had buried themselves deep in her flesh, raking it open with their downward sweep. Her jacket and sari were torn to pieces, and she lay in a welter of blood, blissfully unconscious after her experience.

I saw at once that such meagre first-aid equipment as I had was totally inadequate to meet the situation, but we quickly washed the wounds with strong solution of potassium permanganate and roughly bandaged her chest and abdomen with strips torn from another sari. Her father, two brothers, and three willing men from the village then carried her on a rope-cot to the Studebaker. Placing her as comfortably as possible in the 'dickie', I took her three male relations aboard and set out for the town of Kankanhalli, which boasted the nearest village hospital. We reached there after three-thirty in the morning, when I awoke the doctor and handed over the injured woman. Her condition appeared to be very low, owing to the great deal of blood she had lost.

By four-thirty, I was in the bathroom of the traveller's bungalow at Kankanhalli, where I removed my blood-soaked clothing and took a cold bath. I had no change of clothing with me, having left them behind at Sangam in the confusion of the moment. So I borrowed a clean *dhoti* and a blanket from the bungalow-waiter.

Dawn was breaking when I knocked at the Post Office, awoke a most obliging postmaster from his sleep, paid the necessary late fee and despatched an urgent telegram to Bangalore requesting extension of leave for four more days.

When I returned to the bungalow I found the younger brother of the injured woman awaiting me in tears. He had come from the hospital to tell me his sister had just died. Shortly afterwards, the father came to ask me to take his daughter's body back in the car to Sangam for cremation by the banks of the river Cauvery, in which the ashes would eventually be scattered. It was a request I could not refuse. The bungalow servant told me he wanted his *dhoti* and blanket back. So I had to dress again in my blood-smeared clothes.

We drove back to the hospital, placed the still, limp body of the girl in the back seat, and set out on the return journey to Sangam, delayed by two hours at the Police Station, where we reported the occurrence.

After a bath in a quiet pool beside the river, free from crocodiles, a change into fresh clothing, a cold lunch and two big mugs of tea, I lay back in a rickety old armchair to review the situation. My loaded pipe, from which the comforting smoke arose in spirals to the roughly-tiled low roof, helped a great deal to soothe my ragged nerves after the events of the previous night and to prevent my eyes from closing with sleep.

What should I do with the remaining four days and five nights at my disposal, to rid these poor village-folk from another, and still another, and God only knew how many more repetitions of these terrible events. Facts appeared to indicate that: (1) the panther would not take animal baits, (2) it had a wide range of cover, and (3) it was predisposed to dragging people out of huts. Then, while I pondered, I fell asleep.

At 3 p.m. I awoke and a possible line of action appeared to have presented itself while I slept. It was this:

The small village of Sangam, with about a dozen huts, had been constructed in the usual fashion, on both sides of a central lane. I remembered that on the southern side of this lane, and not far from the river bank, small herds of cattle belonging to the villagers were corralled in a common enclosure, surrounded by a fence of bamboo, intersticed with cut lantana brambles. The only dogs left in the village, which had belonged to the man who had been killed, were enclosed in the shed-like room where he had been slain, which room happened to adjoin the larger cattle enclosure on its western side. The idea came to me that, if I posted myself at night in the midst of the cattle, not only would I be perfectly safe from unexpected attack, as the cattle would grow restive and give ample warning should the panther approach, but this very restlessness, and the fact that the dogs too would join in the alarm, would help me to learn of the panther's presence, should he enter the village. Meanwhile, I would keep my five live baits tied out on the off-chance that one of them might be taken instead.

With this plan in view, I dressed warmly for the night, wearing a khaki woollen 'balaclava' cap to keep off the dew. My usual night equipment included, this time a large flask of tea, some biscuits, and my pipe, as I knew that smoking, in this case, would do no harm.

Because of the panther's presence, the villagers were inside their huts, behind doors barricaded and reinforced with freshly-cut thorns, long before six o'clock. I took up my position in the middle of the cattle enclosure. About me was a space of about fifty yards in every direction, with nearly hundred nondescript cattle scattered around.

At fist the animals resented my presence and crowded to the corners away from me, leaving me isolated in the centre of the pen. I started trying to make friends with them. One kicked over my flask of tea and nearly broke it! Moreover, some of the bulls were rather truculent and made short jabs at me with their horns if I came too close. After an hour in each other's company, the situation eased a little, and I was able to make my way guardedly to the centre of the herd, about half of whom were now resting on the ground. I got down also.

As the hours dragged by, the silence was unbroken, except for an occasional snort from one of the animals, or the trampling of another as it altered its position. One cow became friendly and insisted in nuzzling her muzzle against my chest as a gesture of companionship. Eventually she flopped down contentedly on the ground beside me.

Then cattle-ticks began to bite me in many places and mercilessly. I scratched myself vigorously, although I knew that by doing so I would only increase the irritation. It grew colder, and soon I was glad to nuzzle myself, in my turn, up against the warm body of the cow who had chosen to open this strange friendship with me. Now and again, one of the herd would 'moo' contentedly, or snort, or kick, or flop down to the ground, or struggle to its feet.

The hours still dragged by, and the ticks continued to bite. At one o'clock a sambar belled on the small hill to the north of the village. It was a doe that had called, and she called again and again. Then her call was taken up by a kakar, whose hoarse bark resounded across the *nullahs* which furrowed the lower slopes of the hillock.

THE SANGAM PANTHER

The sambar doe had stopped belling by this time, while the kakar climbed up, giving occasional vent to his guttural call. Whatever it was that had alarmed them had come down the hill.

Some twenty minutes later spotted deer began their warning cries, answering one another from the jungle that slopes from the base of the hill to the edge of the river. Either a tiger or a panther was afoot, and the next few minutes would tell whether the carnivore was just a normal animal or the marauder I was awaiting.

It was almost pitch-dark when the cattle grew restless. With one accord, those lying on the ground scrambled to their feet, and I did the same, keeping close beside the friendly cow. Some of the bulls snorted, and the herd were all turned towards the lane that divided the small village and passed by the thorn hedge that bordered the cattle stockade.

The animals became very restless and began to gather in a mass at the further end of the stockade, away from the hedge and lane. The four dogs in the neighbouring shed had been barking furiously; they now began to whimper. Whatever had frightened them was passing down that lane at that very moment.

I had got myself wedged in the midst of the cattle and had to watch carefully against being impaled on one of the many horns that were nervously tossing about me. I began to force myself through the herd to reach their front rank, hoping that I might be able to see something, but the darkness and the hedge revealed nothing.

I could hear the dogs howling and whimpering in the shed in which they were locked. My ears were attuned to catch the slightest sound, but the noise made by the cattle and the dogs gave me little chance. Some minutes later, I caught the faintest of scratching noises. Listening carefully I located it as coming from further down the lane. They became louder and more impatient. Then I realised that the panther was scratching at a door of one of the huts some distance away.

Breaking through the remainder of the cattle, I approached the fence on tiptoe, hoping to be able to peep over it and catch a glimpse of the panther when I switched on the torch at the end of my rifle. The inmates of the hut at which the panther was scratching chose that very moment to set up a bedlam of shrieks and shouts; the silence was broken by the most frightful din.

Thinking that the man-eater had succeeded in forcing his way into the hut, I threw discretion to the winds and rushed for the bamboo-and-thorn door that formed the entrance of the stockade. At dusk I had firmly wedged a huge Y-shaped log into place, and it took some precious moments to release its base from the big stones against which I had jammed it.

Dragging it aside and switching on the torch, I heaved the clumsy door back and stepped into the lane. Nothing was to be seen in any direction.

Keeping my back to the thorn fence to guard against attack from the rear, I shone the beam in all directions, but I still saw nothing. The panther had disappeared into thin air. Meanwhile, the shrieks and shouts continued unabated.

Then it occurred to me that perhaps the panther was inside the hut all this time, mauling and killing the inmates, and with this alarming thought in mind I began carefully to cover the intervening twenty yards.

When I came abreast of the entrance, I found it was shut fast. I called out to the inmates. At first, due to the noise they were making, they could not hear me. Then I called again, louder and many times. The the hubbub gradually subsided.

I shouted to the occupants to open the door. They would not do so. Then a tremendous voice from inside asked whether I was a man or a devil. I called back that it was I, and that

THE SANGAM PANTHER

the panther had gone. The voice replied that the inmates would open the door only when morning came. Meanwhile, my torch beam clearly showed the fresh claw-marks on the door of the hut, where the panther had just tried to effect an entrance.

I returned to the stockade, reclosed the door, replaced the Y-shaped log and the stones and went back to the spot where I had been lying against the cow when the alarm had begun.

To my horror, I found that the milling feet of the herd had smashed my thermos and it was now impossible to drink the hot tea for which I longed. My biscuits also had been devoured, and as I watched her ruefully, the friendly cow devoured the last of the paper in which they had been wrapped. Fortunately, I had kept my pipe and tobacco in my pocket, and with this I spent the rest of the night in comparative comfort, once again nestling against the side of the cow.

I returned to the bungalow at dawn, tired and disappointed. Worst of all, my body was a mass of tick-bites and itched abominably. Further, I knew only too well that each bite would fester during the coming ten days, and that I was in for a most uncomfortable time.

A cold bath and change, followed by hot tea, tinned bacon and bread and butter helped to ease my gloom, and by 7.30 a.m. I was asleep. I awoke for lunch at midday, and slept again till 3 p.m. Then I got up and began to work out another plan.

It would be impossible to sit with the cattle again, for if I was to get bitten once more by as many ticks as in the previous night, I might end with a dose of tick fever. Yet it was undeniable that both the cattle and the dogs had helped admirably in giving me the alarm when the panther had passed down the lane.

At last I had a fresh idea, that appeared to be the only compromise in the situation. The roof of the dog-shed consisted of scraps of zinc sheeting. I decided that I would lie on that roof, suitably camouflaged and overlooking the lane, so that I should be able to shoot the panther if it walked down the lane again. The cattle and the dogs would still help me by giving the alarm. I could protect my rear and both flanks by heaping stacks of cut thorns on to the roof. Any heavy body, like the panther, that leapt upon the zinc roof would necessarily give its presence away by the noise that would follow. Not only did this appear to be the only solution, but actually a good solution of the problem.

So I hurried towards the village, carrying my night-kit, biscuits, tea (poured into an empty beer bottle, borrowed from the bungalow watchman). After telling the villagers of my new plan, willing hands soon stacked piles of cut thorn branches on to the zinc roof of the goat-shed in the form of a square. Others brought dried straw, which they placed on the roof within the square of thorns for me to lie on.

At 6 p.m. I took up my position. There were two disadvantages that almost immediately began to show themselves: the first, that having to face the lane all the time, I would have to lie so that my legs would be slightly higher than my head, for the zinc roof sloped slightly downwards from back to front, to allow rain-water to flow off easily; the second, that I would have to remain lying on my stomach for most of the time, since my slightest movement sounded distinctly on the zinc roof. But the advantages were that I was safe from surprise attack from the rear; that I had a clear and unobstructed view of the lane and could hear distinctly, particularly if the cattle or the dogs became uneasy; lastly, that I was away from those awful ticks.

But that night was a peaceful one, without any indication whatever that the panther had come within two or three miles of the village. Back at the bungalow next morning I had another bath, and another daylong sleep. Each day I had had my live baits checked by a group of men, but none of these beasts had been harmed.

That night I took up position on the roof once more. It was past 2 a.m., and there had been no alarms from the surrounding jungle, and I felt very drowsy. Suddenly, as in a dream, I heard the cattle begin to stir restlessly. One of the dogs in the shed beneath me growled. Then all four of them began to bark or howl together.

Peering forward slowly, I began to scan the village lane in both directions. Starlight was not good at that moment, only enough to prevent the night from being obscure. The lane to the right and left appeared as a faint blur and of a slightly lighter shade than the surroundings. I could hear nothing and see nothing.

Then I caught the faintest of sounds. It appeared to be a hiss such as a cobra might make. Yes, there it was again! And it came from in front and directly below me. Was it the hiss of a snake or the faint noise a panther makes when he curls back the skin of his upper lip?

I peered downwards and at first could see nothing. Seconds later a faint elongated shape registered itself on my vision in that difficult light, a smudge of an infinitesimally lighter shade than the surrounding blur of the lane. I stared at it, and thought I saw it move. The hiss was repeated more distinctly this time. It appeared to come from this lighter smudge. The dogs inside the shed below me now started to whine and whimper. The cattle were very restless.

I realised that I could not point my rifle downwards from where I lay, I would have to move forward another foot perhaps, till my head and shoulders completely cleared the edge of zinc sheet on which I was lying. I began to do this, but despite my utmost care, the straw rustled and the zinc creaked faintly.

There came an ominous growl from that lightish smudge, and I knew that I was discovered and that within the next few seconds the panther would probably jump on the zinc roof and on to me.

Kicking myself forward the remaining six inches, I lowered the rifle over the side of the roof and depressed the torch-switch. Two gleaming orbs reflected the light from a spotted body, crouched for the spring. Only a single shot was required at that point-blank range and the spark of life slowly faded from those blazing orbs: from fiery white they became a dull orange, then a faint green, then an empty glimmer, and finally a purplish blue as the light was reflected back by the now lifeless retina.

It was an old female that I saw next morning, with canine teeth worn down almost to their stubs. Her coat was extremely pale; even her rosettes were ill-formed and dull. Her claws were blunt and worn. There appeared to be no other signs of deformity of any sort about her, or indication of an earlier wound. It seemed that only old age, and the prospect of gradual starvation through her physical incapacity to kill animals, had caused the Sangam panther to make war on the human race—a war which, however ghastly and fearsome while it lasts, invariably ends in the death of the feline. Modern firearms and the human intellect are heavy odds against the jungle instinct, cunning and pangs of hunger.

Six

The Ramapuram Tiger

THIS IS THE STORY OF A TIGER THAT FOR THREE MONTHS HELD SWAY over nearly half a district, an area some sixty miles long by another sixty or so broad. Although his reign was comparatively short, it was nevertheless hectic, for during this short time the Ramapuram tiger was literally here, there and everywhere within the 3,600 square miles of his domain. Like the Scarlet Pimpernel he was sought by all, yet found by none, till his end came in an unexpected manner.

The district of North Coimbatore is largely made up of hills and forest. Bounded on the south by the low-lying plains of Coimbatore proper, it rises abruptly to the Dimbum escarpment. On the southwest are the jungles of the Nilgiri or Blue Mountain range. On the west, the forests of Mysore. To the northwest is another high range of hills—the Biligirirangans. North, northeast and eastwards flows the Cauvery river, clothed on both its banks with heavy jungle, the northeastern and eastern portions abutting on the forests of the district of Salem.

There is only one town worthy of that name in the district of North Coimbatore: Kollegal, which lies at the northwestern corner, scarcely eight miles from the Cauvery. Four roads branch out of Kollegal. Those that run westwards and northwards into Mysore play no part in this story. The third leads southwards and is more or less straight and runs along the eastern base of the Biligirirangan hills. Seventeen miles along this road brings one to the large village of Lokkanhalli; thirteen miles beyond Lokkanhalli is Bailur, where the 'Bison Range' begins and reaches to Hasanpur at the forty-eighth milestone, and to Dimbum, at the top of the escarpment, fifty-two miles from Kollegal.

The fourth road leads in a southeasterly direction and cuts through the village of Ramapuram, about twenty-five miles from Kollegal, where it turns southwards and leads to Bargur, twenty-four miles further on, then to Tamarakarai, another five miles, and finally to the southeastern end of the Dimbum escarpment, where it drops sharply to the village of Andiyur on the plains. This road totals about eighty-one miles in length.

The Kollegal-Lokkanhalli-Bailur-Dimbum road carried sparse lorry traffic and a daily bus service; whereas the road to Ramapuram, Tamarakari and Andiyur was unfit for motor traffic, except jeeps or old-fashioned high-clearance American cars, over the last sixty miles of its length. The terrain is fearful, consisting of sharp rising and falling gradients strewn with boulders. It becomes a narrow track, cut deeply by the wheels of bullock-carts and hemmed in on both sides by dense forest. The sandy—and often rocky-beds of forest streams cross and recross this track at intervals. In the deeper valleys vast areas of the mighty bamboo prevail, the drooping stems touching the hood of the car as it labours and chugs along in low gear with its radiator invariably boiling. Occasionally a fallen bamboo stem, or the broken branch of a tree, lies across the track, torn down to appease the ravenous appetite of an elephant. The driver then halts, and with his axe, or 'chopper' as it is here called, cuts away the obstruction and drags it aside, then moves on until he meets another similar obstruction. Without the handy 'chopper', this track would be impassable.

Tigers normally dislike very dense vegetation, and keep to low scrub jungle, but it is preferred by elephants and bison. The tiger has various reasons for its preference, one being that almost impenetrable undergrowth prevents the tiger from carefully stalking his prey and hinders his terribly effective last-minute charge. Another reason is that the tiger's legitimate prey — deer of all kinds, wild pig and, of course, village cattle — do not enter very dense jungle, which is mainly inhabited by elephants and bison of which the tiger generally keeps clear. A third reason is that thick undergrowth harbours insect pests, such as leeches, many species of animal-ticks, and the horse or animal fly, as it is called in India; tigers have a great aversion to these pests.

The Ramapuram man-eater was reported to have come from the banks of the Cauvery river, from the region of a mountain known as Ponnachai Malai, over six thousand feet in altitude. A few minor coffee-estates, owned by Sholagas and other Indian planters, exist on the slopes of this mountain. It is said that the Ramapuram man-eater began his career as an ordinary cattle-lifter that made a habit of raiding these estates for what he could pick up in the way of domestic cattle belonging to the planters and the coolies. He is reported to have killed and eaten several cattle, till one planter, more enterprising than his fellows, went down to Coimbatore city and purchased a gin-trap of truly formidable appearance.

MAN-EATERS AND JUNGLE KILLERS

This trap was made of iron with two semicircular rows of teeth, which when opened and held apart, had a spread of almost two-and-a-half feet. The teeth were about two inches long. The jaws were kept apart by a hair-trigger arrangement, which, when released, allowed an exceptionally powerful spring to bring the jaws noisily together at lightning speed, so that the wicked teeth meshed with each other.

Soon afterwards, the tiger killed a milch-cow which it dragged into a ravine and concealed beneath a heap of dried leaves, without starting to feed. The kill was followed and discovered, and the trap was carefully set near the hindquarters of the cow, at which place the tiger would normally start operations when he returned for his meal. The same dried leaves that concealed the kill were used to hide the trap. The tiger returned, and to his bad luck and the future ill-fortune of others—got his head in the trap, which caught him firmly on both sides of the neck, just behind the ears.

The trap had been anchored to the ground with a stake. The tiger tore at the trap and succeeded in uprooting the stake, while the jaws held firm in his neck. He then rushed away into the jungle, dragging the heavy trap with him, till at a spot almost two miles distant the trap got itself firmly wedged between two big rocks. The tiger tried to drag itself free, but only succeeded in wedging the trap more firmly than before.

The tiger roared with pain, and struggled desperately. The roars were heard for half the night by the planter and his frightened coolies, two miles away at their plantation. Finally, the animal broke loose losing its left ear and eye in the process, with very severe injuries to the rest of the neck and face. It was heard in the area moaning with pain night and day for quite a week afterwards.

Then came a period of absolute silence. Everyone thought the tiger had died of its wounds. The planter and his hirelings kept a careful watch for vultures, who would doubtless spot the carcase and betray the whereabouts of the dead animal by swooping to earth for their meal. But the only vultures seen were those soaring in the high heavens, carefully scanning the earth below for the signs of death; but none swooped, for the very good reason that the tiger was not dead.

A fortnight passed; then one afternoon, along the *path* to one of the smaller coffee-estates, climbed Jeyken, a Sholaga, and his eighteen-year-old spouse. In accordance with the established Indian custom, Jeyken walked in front, with the woman about a yard behind him, carrying a sack of grain balanced on her head. They had crossed a dry streambed, and were just climbing its slight embankment, when, out of a clump of grass like sugarcane that grows only along river banks in these areas, a tiger pounced upon the girl, throwing her to the earth.

Turning, Jeyken saw his wife lying on the ground gazing at him with terror-stricken, pleading eyes. The tiger crouched upon her back, its two paws overlapping her shoulders, the wide-open mouth just above her head. It was a tiger with no left eye, and no left ear, while the wounds on its neck and face had not yet healed!

Jeyken was turned to stone. He could not move and he could not speak, but remained rooted to the spot in horror and amazement. The tiger snarled horribly, contorting its already lacerated features into a still more horrible mask. Then it grabbed the girl by her right shoulder and walked across the stream with its prey—the girl hung head downwards, her loose hair and left arm and legs dragging in the sand. A moment later, the tiger and the girl had disappeared in the jungle on the further side.

Evidently the poor woman had swooned, or may already have died of fright. That was the last Jeyken ever saw of his wife, nor had she uttered the slightest cry, even at the moment of attack.

A month later a herd-boy was killed by a tiger within two miles of Ramapuram. In this case the half-eaten remains were found in a bush. The third human kill occurred about three weeks later, almost at the twenty-first milestone on the Kollegal-Lokkanhalli-Bailur-Dimbum road. This time it was a road-coolie, a middle-aged woman, who was attacked in full view of her companions just before five in the evening. She had stopped work for a few minutes, and had gone some yards into the jungle, when a tiger pounced upon her as if from nowhere and carried her away. She had screamed frenziedly, and those who were in the vicinity had clearly seen the tiger. It had a scarred face and no left ear or eye!

It so happened that my game licence for the North Coimbatore area had at that time expired. This area is divided into two forest divisions: North Coimbatore proper and the Kollegal Division. For although Kollegal fell within North Coimbatore district for administrative purposes, the Forest department had recently subdivided the district into two distinct Forest Divisions. My licence, which had expired, covered North Coimbatore proper and Dimbum; while Lokkanhalli, Bailure and Ramapuram fell within the Kollegal Division. I had intended renewing my old licence, and was about to send the required fee when I read in the papers about the latest outrage committed by this tiger. That decided me, and with ten days' privilege leave at my disposal, I left Bangalore early in the morning, reaching the Forest department office at Kollegal, eighty-seven miles away, even before it had opened for the day. It did not take me long to get the required shooting licence, and all available information regarding the tiger.

The area where the man-eater had operated was comparatively new to me, so I decided, for a start, to camp

THE RAMAPURAM TIGER

in the small forest lodge at Ramapuram, twenty-five miles away, which I reached in an hour and a half, after negotiating an extremely bumpy road.

Obviously, the first thing to do was to try and win the confidence of the inhabitants of Ramapuram by telling them I had come to try to rid them of the tiger. The people did not know me and gave somewhat garbled accounts, indicating that the tiger might be anywhere between Ponnachai Malai, where it had struck down it first victim, and Bailur, a distance of about sixty miles as the crow flies.

Bailur, as I have told you, was a small village some thirty miles from Kollegal, on the Kollegal-Lokkanhalli-Dimbum road. Thus, I could either return to Kollegal by car and motor thence to Bailur, or I could leave the car at Ramapuram and cover the third side of the triangle by walking from Ramapuram to Bailur, a distance of nearly nineteen miles. I decided to follow the latter course, as it would give me the opportunity of passing through several Forest hamlets bordering the Reserved Forest, where I hoped to get some news of the tiger.

Accordingly, at dawn next morning I left the little Forest Lodge at Ramapuram and began my walk to Bailur. The *path* led in a generally southwesterly direction, alternatively through sparsely cultivated country and scrub jungle, which skirted the ranges of small hills lying a couple of miles southward, within the boundaries of the Reserved Forest proper.

I passed a few hamlets, but all the inhabitants were either indoors or squatting at the entrances of their huts. Their few cattle were kraaled outside or grazed at will on the scant herbage in the immediate vicinity of the huts, for the story of the man-eater had spread far and wide and the usual scare that attends such visitations had already set in.

I walked slowly making inquiries wherever possible. Almost all the Sholagas inhabiting these hamlets reported that they had heard a tiger roaring in the vicinity, either the previous night or within the past seventy-two hours. At one spot I was shown the clear pug-marks of a tiger as it had crossed a recently ploughed field, just a hundred yards from the owner's hut. I took detailed measurements of those pugs for future reference before moving on but it soon became evident that the people in this area were either so nervous that they were making completely false and exaggerated reports, or else that an unusual number of tigers were operating along the nineteen miles between Ramapuram and Bailur. For, according to the information obtained, a tiger appeared to have visited each hamlet within the last three or four days!

At about 5 p.m. I approached Bailur, a village of some twenty huts. Here I met members of the road gang who had witnessed the killing of the woman near the twenty-first milestone. They told me what I have already recorded and particularly stressed the tiger's deformities, which they had all clearly seen while they stood rooted to the spot with terror, while the tiger made off into the undergrowth with its still-screaming victim, the road-coolie woman.

The nearest Forest department Lodge was some three-and-a-half miles farther along the motor-road in the direction of Dimbum. The Reserve lay along both sides of the road. It was now 5.30 p.m., and I knew that night would fall in an hour, so I covered those last three-and-a-half miles at a brisk pace, reaching the little Forest Bungalow shortly before dark.

The sun had gone down behind the towering range of the Biligirirangan Hills, which lay some three miles west of the bungalow, and the twilight calls of roosting peacock and junglefowl welcomed me as I sank into an old broken armchair which I dragged on to the verandah. The distant challenge of a sambar stag, descending the western range, was music to my ears as it floated across the dense valley separating the

THE RAMAPURAM TIGER

bungalow from the foothills. The myriad tree-tops of this valley were like a dark carpet in the deepening twilight.

Scarcely half-an-hour had passed before total darkness prevailed, punctuated by the incessant flicker of a million fireflies. They floated everywhere, like tiny elfin spirits in the gloom, carrying their lanterns of pinpoint brilliance to every bush tree-top in the vicinity. At rare intervals their flashes would synchronise, and the tree or bush around which they clustered would throb and pulsate to one big and unanimous flash of light, made by thousands of these little creatures. The blackness of the jungle night would disperse before a phosphorescent and ethereal glow—but only for a moment—until that rare interval of synchronisation occurred again.

I made an early night of it, sleeping on the floor of the small central room of the lodge; but at about 2 a.m., the moaning call of a tiger woke me. I heard it call at intervals as it traversed the valley, until it died away in the distance.

Early morning found me back in Bailur village, where I enlisted the help of two local *shikaris* and purchased three young bulls for bait. One of these we tethered in the bed of the stream that traversed the valley west of the bungalow, where I had heard the tiger calling in the night. The second was tied in a small forest-glade a bare 100 yards from the roadside, midway between the village and the Forest Bungalow. To tie the third, we walked back to the twenty-first milestone, where the road-worker had been killed. Close to this spot the road was crossed by a forest stream, known as Oddam Betta Halla; its banks were clothed with bamboo, except for a small clearing made by the Forest department, in which seedlings of various forest plants were being experimentally grown. My helpers told me that a tiger often walked through this clearing, and I found this statement to be true, in that pug-marks both old and comparatively new were visible at three different place. I examined the most recent of these imprints, and compared them with the measurements of the pug-marks taken at the hamlet on the previous day. Both sets had been made by a male tiger, but those in the departmental plantation belonged to a much older and heavier animal.

We tied the third bait on open ground just where the Oddam Betta Halla stream flows past this plantation.

When all this had been done it was 5.30 p.m., and on our return to Bailur village I was approached by a sturdy, good-looking Sholaga, who introduced himself as Jeyken, the husband of the girl who had been the man-eater's first victim. He said that a party of travellers who had passed by the coffee estate on the slopes of Ponnachai Malai, where he worked, had informed him that a *Sahib* had come to Ramapuram to shoot the tiger. Filled with the idea of revenge for his wife's murder, he had obtained the planter's permission to go to Ramapuram to offer me his assistance. At Ramapuram he was told that I had gone to Bailur, whither he had immediately followed me, all by himself.

I thanked Jeyken for his offer, and the trouble he had taken to find me, and immediately recruited him as my personal helper. I liked his appearance and his calm determination to leave no stone unturned to bring the tiger to book. Jeyken smiled at my acceptance and thanked me in turn, but he staunchly refused to accept any payment; indeed, he made it abundantly clear that this was the condition of his offer.

I returned to the Forest Lodge, instructing Jeyken and the other two helpers to make an early start next morning and visit the bait near the twenty-first milestone. For myself, I would visit the other two baits. This I did next morning, first visiting the bull tethered on the streambed in the valley, then the bait that was tied midway between the Forest bungalow and Bailur village. Both were unharmed and no traces of pugs were to be seen in any sand that existed near the spots where they were tied. I then walked the remaining distance to Bailur village, where I awaited the return of my three scouts; within an hour they arrived, to tell me the third bait was alive.

Leaving Jeyken and one of the Sholagas at the village, I took the second man, who claimed to be well acquainted with the forest gamepaths in that area, and walked westwards till we entered the foothills of the Biligirirangans. As all this area was unfamiliar to me, I got him to walk in front, while I covered him from the rear with my rifle ready in my hands. Sholagas are born jungle folk, and my guide showed no signs of nervousness while we threaded our way thus, in single file, up one game-path and down another, across dark *nullahs*, often bending double to avoid overhanging fronds of bamboo or outcrops of wait-a-bit thorn. But no signs of a fresh tiger track did we see.

A large male panther had crossed at one spot, and at another spot a female, accompanied by her cub; but it was evident that the tiger we were looking for had not passed that way.

It was nearing 3 p.m. before we got back to the Forest Lodge and a late cold lunch. The Sholaga made a fire, on which I boiled some water to brew us several cups of tea. Then I drew water from the little well in the compound, to give myself the luxury of a cold bath.

At five I returned with the Sholaga to Bailur village, where I left him with instructions for Jeyken, himself and the third Sholaga to visit the bait on the twenty-first milestone early next morning. It was well past seven by the time I got back to the bungalow. I slept soundly that night, nor did the moaning call of any tiger disturb me. Early morning found me on my way to visit the other two baits. Both were unharmed.

Returning to the Forest Lodge, I ate a frugal meal and then walked towards Bailur, carefully watching the road for pug-marks. No tiger had passed that way and 9.15 a.m. found me awaiting my henchmen. They returned before ten, this time to report that the bait had been killed and removed by a tiger, which had contrived to bite through the tethering rope.

Fortunately I had come prepared for such an eventuality and had brought my torch and other night-shooting kit with me in a haversack. Back we went as fast as we could, and shortly after midday had reached the spot where the bull had been tied. The tiger's pug-marks, in approaching the bait, were apparent in the soft earth some twenty feet away, and an examination showed that the killer was a tigress and not a tiger. From there she had launched her final attack that had killed the bull, biting through the rope by which its leg had been tied.

We could not know how far the kill had been taken, so I told my companions to wait for me by the twenty-first milestone till 3 p.m., while I would follow the drag-mark. If the dead bull had been taken for some distance, I would try to build myself a hide-out to await the return of the tigress, and would make it an all-night affair. Under such circumstances, I would not be back by three and they were to return to Bailur. On the other hand, if the tigress had dropped the kill not far away, I would return to my companions and get them to put up a proper *machan*.

I found the tigress had half-dragged the kill for the first two hundred yards, by which time she had got clear of the bamboo jungle that grew on the lower land and in the vicinity of the stream. Then she had encountered some heavy lantana undergrowth, which had obviously been an obstruction to her passage, encumbered as she was with the dead bull. Here she had evidently slung it over her shoulder, as tigers sometimes do to carry their kills, and it then became extremely difficult to follow the trail.

A dragging hoof, or the horns of the bull, had here and there broken a twig, and these were the only visible signs of passage. The carpet of rotting vegetation, and fallen lantana leaves, effectively did away with any hope of finding pug-marks. Necessarily, the going was also very slow, nor did I like the situation at all, as almost my whole attention had to be given to following the trail, which prevented me from being fully on my guard against a sudden attack. Finally the lantana gave way to more open forest, sprinkled liberally with trees and a carpet of the dwarf date palm.

Twice I came across the spot where the tigress had laid down her burden and then picked it up again. It was now evident that she had some particular destination in view, most probably a lair where she had cubs to whom she was taking the meat.

Up and up led the trail; the terrain became more and more rocky, till finally, in a break among the tree-trunks, I saw a hillock, perhaps a quarter-of-a-mile beyond and about 200 feet above the spot where I stood. The trail led directly toward the hillock. By now I felt reasonably certain that the animal I was following was not the man-eater, because all the data gathered about the man-eater had classed it as a tiger and not a tigress, although the sex factor was not an established certainty. As it was a known fact, however, that the man-eater had lost its left eye and ear, if I could but catch a glimpse of the animal I was following, I would soon know whether it was the right one or not.

How to catch that glimpse was the problem. The obvious answer to it was to keep advancing till we met, but it was scarcely to my liking, as even if the tigress was not the man-eater, she certainly was unlikely to welcome any human being who knocked at the door of the lair where she had her cubs.

But I went forward. The trail was now easier to follow, as the tigress had brushed against boulders and rocks, where smears of blood betrayed the passage of the dead bull.

Half the distance was covered now; the other half would bring me to the summit. The boulders lay in heaps, and the trail I was following wound in and out between them, as the tigress picked her *path* to avoid any part of her burden becoming jammed between the rocks. It was ten minutes to three; the sun beat down mercilessly on the bare rocks, which in turn threw the heat back in my face as from the door of a furnace. My clothes were soaked with perspiration, which ran in rivers down my face, getting into my eyes, which burned and smarted, and into the corners of my mouth. I licked my lips and I remember that almost unconsciously, in the excitement of the moment, I noted the salty taste.

My rubber boots made no sound as I negotiated the heated rocks. One corner after another was turned, and at each turn I knew what lay beyond. Then I came upon a shelving rock which met the rising ground at an angle of perhaps three hundred forming a shallow recess rather than a real cave. Two large balls of russet brown, striped with black, white underneath, were tumbling over one another in a vigorous game of 'catch-as-catch-can'. They were two tiger cubs, and they were playing!

I stopped in my tracks; the only movement being an imperceptible cocking of the rifle, with the faintest of clicks. But it was enough! Although they were only cubs, generations of instinct were behind them. They stopped playing, disentangled themselves, and looked at me in alarm.

Even now, I can picture the scene: one cub with a look of innocent surprise, and the other with its features wrinkled to emit a hiss of consternation.

THE RAMAPURAM TIGER

That hiss was the signal for all hell to break loose, for it awoke the tigress, who was sleeping. With a series of shattering roars she dashed out of the cavern, vaulted over the cubs and came straight at me.

The distance may have been twenty yards. I covered her between the eyes as she advanced. Then five yards away she stopped; she crouched with her belly to ground, eyes blazing and mouth wide, while her roars and snarls shook the very ground on which I stood. She was a perfect specimen but certainly not the man-eater!

Wonder of wonders, she had not charged home. Her courage had failed her at the last moment. She was telling me, in the simplest of languages: 'Get out quickly, and don't harm my cubs or I will kill you.'

I was glad to oblige. Step by step, I retreated backwards, while never removing my eyes from hers, never allowing the rifle sights to waver in the slightest, my forefinger still on the trigger.

And she remained where she was! It was as if she understood that I was going. I realised at that moment that she did not want to harm me; that she was only protecting her cubs. Perhaps she was afraid. I was afraid too! But I did not want to harm her, nor destroy that lovely happy little family.

So I continued to retreat backwards. The tigress continued to roar. Now I had turned the corner of the first rock that hid her from view. Only then did I dare to take a hasty glance backwards, to see where I was walking, although I still faced towards the tigress, who had now stopped roaring, but was still growling. I knew that, as long as she continued to make those sounds I was safe; I would know where she was.

Another big boulder was passed; then I turned and beat a hasty retreat before she had time to change her mind and come after me. She stopped growling, and I knew that the real danger had come. She might have gone back to her cubs, or she might be following. I made down the hill as rapidly as possible, glancing frequently behind me. Soon I came to the trees and the date palms, then the lantana belt, up which I had so laboriously followed the trail, and finally to the bamboos and the road.

It was 4.30 p.m. and as instructed, my companions had returned to Bailur. I had nine miles to cover, and only two hours before darkness fell. Nevertheless, I sat by the roadside for five minutes to enjoy a quick smoke. I felt I deserved it. I was thankful, too, that I had not been forced to shoot the tigress, for the sight of those two cubs was still fresh in my memory.

It was past six-thirty before I reached Bailur village. There my three companions awaited me, eager to hear my story. When I had told it, they agreed that it was unusual for a tigress to have failed to press home her charge.

Darkness had set in by the time I left the little village on the last lap of my journey to the forest bungalow. But as one of our baits was tied at a point about half-way between the village and the bungalow in a glade not far from the road, it occurred to me that I would pay it a visit. Why this idea came to me, I cannot tell particularly as I had already looked at it that morning on my way to Bailur. It was an impulse, and I have spent my life responding to impulses. I turned off along the little footpath that led away from the road towards the clearing where the bait was tied. It was quite dark, except for the diffused glow from the stars that shone brightly in a clear blue-black sky. The bushes around me assumed ghostly shapes, and the wind sighed fitfully among the branches of the 'rain-tree' that bordered the road. Now and again, a large teak-leaf fluttered to the ground with the softest of sounds, like some huge moth of the night settling down to rest.

THE RAMAPURAM TIGER

I came up to the small wild-fig tree beneath which my bait was tied. The shadows were deeper there, and the bait was, moreover, a brown one. I could not see it till I came very close, when it lumbered to its feet, as if startled at my approach, even as I was startled by its sudden action. It was still unharmed. I walked around it to the other side, to inspect the rope that held it by the hind leg, in case it had become twisted.

And at that moment the man-eater charged.

It was fortunate for me that I had moved to the other side of the bull, which consequently came between me and the tiger. But I confess that I was taken totally by surprise.

There was tremendous 'Woof' from the jungle from which I had just emerged. The bull swung round. I leaped behind it, with my back to the trunk of the fig tree almost tripping over the tethering rope. A huge grey shape vaulted on to the back of the bull, which collapsed beneath the sudden weight.

But the tiger had not seized the neck or throat. It had simply leaped upon the bull in order to reach me beyond it. Luckily, in falling the bull ruined the tiger's spring, which otherwise would have followed within a split second.

The tiger was extricating itself from the heaving body of the fallen bull when my bullet smashed between its eyes. Convulsively it twisted backwards, still lying across the bull, which now staggered to its feet with the tiger over its back, the head and forequarters sagging forwards.

Automatically, and without thinking, I fired my second shot at a spot which I judged to be behind the tiger's left shoulder. The bull collapsed! The tiger rolled off the bull and towards me, as my third shot took it in the throat.

The bull never moved. The tiger kicked convulsively. And then at last all was still.

The light from the torch on the rifle revealed that my first bullet had smashed the tiger's skull. My second had been too low. The heavy .405 missile had ploughed through the end of the tiger's chest and blown a tremendous hole in the bull's side. My third bullet, a quite unnecessary one, had passed through the tiger's throat, leaving a gaping hole. But I had killed the poor bull that had unwittingly saved my life.

My hands were trembling, my knees wobbled, and suddenly I felt very, very sick. The reaction, after the events of that evening, was sudden. I sat on the ground, with may back to the fig tree, and raised my hand to my forehead, which I was surprised to find icy cold to my touch.

How long I remained thus I do not know. Then I groped for my pipe, filled and lit it. The first few puffs steadied my badly-shaken nerves and I was soon able to get back to the road and retrace my steps to Bailur Village.

I found the inhabitants gathered in the streets, agog with excitement and anticipation. For the surrounding hills had carried the sound of my three shots, which had reverberated across the valleys and stony ridges. They had guessed I had been attacked on the way to the bungalow, but were wondering whether it had been by the man-eater, or some bear or elephant.

Seeing me emerge from the gloom, they rushed forward to welcome me, my three servants well to the fore. I sat down by the roadside and told them the story. Gasps of amazement and incredulity broke from their lips, to be followed by congratulations and a fervent expression of thanks for my safety.

A 'chattie' of fresh hot milk was set before me, and a bunch of bananas. As gifts go, it was not much, but it conveyed the heartfelt thanks of the villagers.

In another half-hour practically the whole village had assembled with lanterns and kerosene torches, a stout pole and coils of rope, to bring in the tiger. Back we went to the spot and over fifty people surveyed the strange scene, their eyes wide open with amazement. Jeyken was especially pathetic to watch. With his knife he started to stab the dead tiger—to my dismay, for he was doing further damage to a skin already well-nigh ruined by my bullets. Gently, but firmly, I drew him off; then he began to weep unrestrainedly, thinking of his dead wife.

The deep-hearted weeping of a strong and brave man is not pleasant to witness; it is infectious, and I felt a strange lump rising in my own throat—a lump which refused to subside for quite a time.

Not much remains to be told, except for a strange sequel. Next morning, when coming to the bungalow, Jeyken passed the spot where I had left the road the previous night. Fifty yards further on he decided to answer a call of nature and stepped behind a star-plum bush for the purpose. There he discovered for the first time that the tiger had been lying in wait for me the previous night; evidently it had been in the vicinity, and had either seen or heard me approaching along the road.

Jeyken told me what he had discovered, and I walked back with him to check it for myself. I found what he said was true. There clearly impressed on the soft sand, were tiger's pug-marks while the soft grass and rank weeds beneath the star-plum bush were still partly flattened by the weight of the tiger's body, although more than twelve hours had passed since he had lain there in ambush, awaiting my approach.

Yet some people tell me that there is no such thing as Providence, a guiding-spirit, intuition, or a sixth sense; call it what you will. I find it more difficult to understand the disbelievers than understand Providence itself!

Seven

The Great Panther of Mudiyanoor

MUDIYANOOR IS THE NAME OF A SMALL VILLAGE NESTLING NEAR THE southeastern end of a fertile valley that lies north of the Moyar river and the frowning crags of the Blue Mountains or Nilgiri range, and south of the foothills of the smaller mountain chain known as the Biligirirangans.

This little valley comes as near as possible on this troubled earth to the elusive 'happy valleys' of fiction, or of which we dream during our restless slumbers. Certain it is that rainfall is assured, even in a season of weak monsoons, due to the abutting mountain ranges at either end. The earth is very fertile, being particularly rich in leaf-mould and a fine red loam, for it was until recent years part of the primeval forest which is slowly, but ever steadily, being pushed back by the inroads of civilisation. The climate is temperate during the days and rather chilly at night, due to the cool breezes that blow down the mountain ridges.

THE GREAT PANTHER OF MUDIYANOOR

Most of the people of Mudiyanoor are farmers, although a few are cattle-grazers, who maintain vast herds of animals which are driven during daylight into the surrounding forest for grazing. The milk from these animals is entirely used in the manufacture of 'ghee' which is simply melted butter, and is employed for cooking throughout India. Kerosene tins, filled with this stuff, are sent up the ghat, as the winding cart-track up the hillside is called, till it meets the main road from Mysore to Satyamangalam at the little hamlet of Dimbum. There the tins of ghee are loaded on to cart—and sometimes lorries—and taken away for sale. There are good markets for it in Mysore and Satyamangalam, and particularly in the more distant town of Gobichettipalayam.

So the population is happy and prosperous. Few strangers visit the valley, because the cart-track is practically unmotorable.

The herds occasionally suffer from a marauding tiger or panther: at other times the farmers awake to find sections of their fields trampled flat by elephants which have fed there during the night. Wild pigs and deer take a moderate toll of crops, but these are considered minor calamities and are accepted as the dictates of inevitable fate.

The 'great panther' earned that name because he was quite outstandingly large. He was suspected of having come from the fastnesses of the Blue Mountains, perhaps from Anaikutty or Segur, and across the Moyar river, or Mysore Ditch as it is more commonly called. He began his depredations on the village cattle, killing in true tiger style by breaking the neck, and was therefore mistaken for that animal for some time.

Then, with increasing boldness, this panther started to harry the herds of fine milch cows that were part of my friend Hughie Hailstone's estate. This estate, the Moyar Valley Ranch, is an outstanding farm which is natural, for its owner is an outstanding character. A brilliant engineer by profession, he has the quick brain of an inventor—quick at thinking and quick at assessing values—and from his cleverness have originated many devices and mechanical improvements. In addition, Hughie is a born *shikari*. He loves the forest and its animals, and he is never happier than when handling, or tinkering with, a firearm. From this rare combination of mechanical genius and a love of the wild, Moyar Valley Ranch was born; for with herculean effort and skill, tenacity of purpose and the will to surmount all obstacles, Hughie literally carved his ranch out of the heart of the virgin jungle.

Mighty forest trees had to be cut down and cleared. Hughie exploited this circumstance by converting them into charcoal, which he then sold by lorry-loads to the far distant towns. Bricks, cut-stones, cement, mortar, and all the other items used in building construction had to be brought from the same places. Carpenters were also imported, who, under Hughie's able directions, soon utilised the better forest-woods for building purposes. A modern building rose in no time. With a windmill battery-charger, the house had electric lighting, a refrigerator and many up-to-date conveniences. In addition, farm machinery was imported, so that in almost the twinkling of an eye Moyar Valley Ranch became a flourishing farmstead.

Hughie has many business interests and frequently travels abroad. Sometimes he returns in a few weeks, but at others he is absent for months, and the following story concerns one of his long absences. He had very kindly offered me the privilege of visiting his farm at any time, and has especially asked me to keep a watchful eye on his livestock. So one day, when we received a letter from Hugh's caretaker, a man named Varghese, that the big panther had killed Hugh's finest Alsatian, something had to be done.

THE GREAT PANTHER OF MUDIYANOOR

At that time I was immersed in some heavy and urgent work and it was impossible to get away for the next fortnight. Varghese's letter, having travelled by village post, had already taken six days to reach us. But my son Donald volunteered to deal with the panther, and I gladly delegated this job to him. The Studebaker had broken an axle a month earlier and I was still awaiting a replacement from Bombay, so Donald rushed off to his friend's house to borrow a car.

From this point I feel I had better let Donald relate the rest of the story himself, as I took no further part in the affair, beyond giving him a piece of my mind when he returned from the expedition.

'When Dad told me to go to Mudiyanoor, the first problem was to find a car to travel by, as his Studebaker was laid up. So I thought of a friend who had been with me at school, named Rustam Dudhwala. Rustam is a nice fellow and owns three or four cars. So with a bit of sales talk I had no difficulty in getting him interested. It took me just four hours to get together the odds and ends necessary for the trip, and to borrow Dad's lucky tiger-charm, which was given to him years ago by a jungle man named Budhia. I know Dad does not talk about this charm, as he thinks people will make fun of him, but I also know that he appears to have much faith in it. The charm is actually wrapped in a small piece of bamboo, tied with a strand of hair from an elephant's tail. What is inside it I do no know. The whole thing can be worn around the neck, as the bamboo is tied to a piece of string, but Dad generally stuffs it into his pocket.

'Just before leaving I thought of taking another friend along with me, a fellow named Cedric Bone, who is a keen photographer and good sport, and can rough it out splendidly. Cedric was ready to come, and soon the three of us were on our way to Mudiyanoor. I carried my .423 Mauser, which is a far superior weapon to Dad's old-fashioned .405 Winchester. He knows this himself, but like all old-fashioned people prefers to stick to something that is out of date. I also brought my .3006 Springfield as a reserve rifle for shooting deer for the pot. My old man lectures me against killing deer and I pretend to listen to him. When he is around, of course, such killing is taboo; but when he is not there it is quite a different matter.

'The last seventeen miles of the track to Mudiyanoor is really bad, and it took us almost eight hours to get there. Varghese greeted me with a broad smile, although I felt he was a little disappointed because Dad had not come along. That is the trouble nowadays. Young people like me are often not appreciated and the older men seem to regard us as being somewhat irresponsible. They forget that they too were young once.

'Anyhow, Varghese told us that, apart from village cattle, the big panther had also killed a cow belonging to Mr. Hailstone three days ago. The immediate problem was therefore to buy some live bait in the form of half-grown bulls, and for this purpose Rustam came in very handy.

'Let me tell you something about this Rustam. He is twenty-two years old and a Parsee, which community are the descendants of early Persian settlers in India. He comes of a very rich family, who owns lakhs of rupees worth of property in Bombay, bringing in enough income in a single day to buy me several times over. Apart from this, Rustam's Dad is a shrewd businessman, who earns an income even larger than what comes in each month from the property. He is a very sporting chap and very fond of his son, but sometimes he gets unreasonably strict about letting Rustam go shooting. When that happens, Rustam and I generally contrive to invite my father to visit Mr. Dudhwala, for when these old men meet and talk things over for an hour or two, our hunting trip is assured.

'Well, to return to what I was telling you. Rustam bought four young bulls, which we tied out in different places near where the big panther had recently killed. The first of these we tied near the forest boundary line which runs beside Mr. Hailstone's estate. The second we tied about a quarter of a mile away, near a small lake surrounded by heavy bamboo jungle. The third we tied on the outskirts of Mudiyanoor village proper, and the last on the cart track itself, coming into Mudiyanoor. Dad always makes a practice of setting up his *machan* along with the baits; but as Varghese had offered the use of Mr. Hailstone's portable *machan*, I decided to set mine up only after a kill had occurred.

'We took care to secure our baits by tying the hind legs to stout stakes driven into the ground, for it is a mistake to pass a rope around the neck of a live bait. Sometimes panthers, and tigers especially, are reluctant to attack an animal with a rope around its neck. They kill by grabbing the neck, and they feel suspicious of a rope, which would get in their way.

'At the last moment Varghese informed us that a tiger had been calling in the vicinity of the bungalow for the past two days. So as an afterthought, instead of a rope I used Mr. Hailstone's chain for securing the bait tied on the forest line near his bungalow. This was because I felt that if the tiger killed this bull he might break the rope and carry it away. As there were no other chains, the other three baits had to remain roped.

'Rustam wanted to go shooting wild pig that night in the fields around Mudiyanoor village, but I stopped him, as a shot might disturb the panther. Next morning, all four of our baits were alive and we were disappointed. But shooting is a game of patience, as Dad has taught me, so I told Rustam to be quiet and not expect developments for another day or two. On the third night the big leopard killed the bull tied on the forest line near the bungalow. It so happened that the tiger also killed the second bait tied among the bamboos near the forest pool the same night.

'Now I was faced with a problem. "Damn the panther," I said to myself "I will get the tiger." But there were other circumstances to be considered: Rustam reminded me that my purpose there was to shoot the panther which had killed Mr. Hailstone's livestock. It was my business, therefore, to sit up for the panther. I knew that he was right and that Dad would say the same. Still, it seemed a bit thick to lose the opportunity of sitting up for the tiger, and I tried hard to persuade Rustam to take on the panther. But he has some of his father's business instincts, and clung to his previous arguments. So, realising I was cornered, I had to give in.

'Cedric elected to come and sit up with me, as he felt that there were more chances of seeing the big panther by being with me, than of seeing the tiger by going with Rustam. He thought Rustam would make too much noise and would drive away the tiger before it ever appeared at the kill.

'So I got to work and had Mr. Hailstone's portable *machan* hung in the tree that grew about thirty yards from the dead bull. Rustam, for his part, got the villagers to erect a *machan* in a tree that grew close to where the other bull had been killed by the tiger. I forgot to mention that, in tying all these four baits, I had taken the precaution of tying them close to trees, so that there would be no trouble later in erecting *machans*.

'Both parties left the bungalow at about 4 p.m. Rustam had a longer distance to cover, so he and Varghese, complete with sandwiches, water bottle, torches, warm mufflers, blankets and what not, started off at a brisk pace. Cedric and I strolled along to the forest line with our packet of food and a single water bottle. We felt blankets were unnecessary as the weather appeared to be warm.

'Sitting in any *machan* is a tiresome business, and I always find it difficult to remain still. My old man has told me many a time that sitting like a graven image is absolutely essential, but how he does it I don't know. I have sat with him often and his style is to fold his legs beneath him, settle himself very comfortably, smoke his pipe, drink a little tea from a flask, and then become a graven image for the rest of the night. But all sorts of things happen to me. I get pins and needles in my feet, my back feels stiff and begins to ache, and the mosquitoes worry me considerably: not only do they bite me, but they find their way into my ears and nose and the only method of getting rid of one is to wait till it settles down to feed, and then give it a smart slap. Dad tells me that this is not the thing to do when on a *machan;* but perhaps he forgets that my blood, being young, is probably more attractive to the mosquitoes than his. You will understand, I am sure, that old men take quite a delight in telling younger people what not to do.

'Anyhow, by the time it grew dark at seven o'clock, these mosquitoes were already very busy on both Cedric and myself. I had already told Cedric to abstain from slapping mosquitoes, which was probably why he nudged me, once or twice, when I did so myself. Time passed, and then, at about a quarter to eight, we saw a longish object, that looked grey in the darkness, appear as if from nowhere. I must explain that, although there was no moon, there was a diffused glow all around from the stars that always seem to twinkle much brighter in a forest. There was enough light, at least, to show up the bigger trees and this grey object, but not the dead bull, which happened to be black. Well, the grey apparition moved towards where the bull lay, and shortly after we heard the rattle of the chain, followed by the sound of eating, and the crunching of bones. Slowly, I raised my rifle to my shoulder, but as luck would have it, my torch, which was fixed to the rifle barrel, struck against the tree and made the slightest of noises. There was a loud growl from the direction of the kill and the same grey object began walking across the forest line towards my left. Soon it disappeared, and then, after about ten minutes, reappeared to my right, but almost beneath us. I heard the sound of licking, and it seemed that the panther was seated there on its haunches. This time I got the rifle levelled properly and pressed the switch of my torch. The bright beam lit the panther, sitting on the ground in a dog-like attitude, hardly twenty yards away, It looked up at me, and taking a quick sight, I pressed the trigger. My best friend, the .432, roared, and the panther fell over sideways. I thought it was done for, but then it suddenly picked itself up again and sprang into the forest below the tree where we were sitting.

'Cedric had been very excited while all this was happening, for no sooner did the panther disappear than he prepared to climb down. I restrained him, and he said, "Come, let's go after it". But I told him not to be a fool and that we had better wait till morning.

'We sat there for nearly another hour. The mosquitoes became so unbearable that we decided to get down and return to the bungalow. I descended first, and Cedric handed me the rifle. Then he followed with the water bottle. The last six feet he took at a jump, and as he hit the ground with a thud there was an awful roar from very near. I swung around, pointing my rifle, with the torch burning, in the direction of the sound, but we could see nothing. After waiting for some minutes, we went forward a few paces, but the lantana undergrowth was very dense here and it seemed unsafe to follow up in the darkness. We then went to the spot where the panther had been seated when I fired, and began to look around for blood.

'There were no traces to be seen by the light of the torch and the alarming idea occurred to me that perhaps I had made a complete miss. I discussed the matter in undertones with Cedric, but he was certain that my bullet had struck the panther. Still, I was doubtful and we eventually decided to go back to the *machan,* on the very slim chance that I might have missed and the panther might later return to its kill.

'The rest of the night was extremely uncomfortable, what with the mosquitoes and the intense cold that began to set in with the early hours of the morning. We stuck it out, however, and dawn found us a very dejected and disappointed pair. We climbed down from the tree and stretched out in the green grass below it for nearly an hour, in order to give the sun a chance to rise, and to relax our stiffened muscles. Then, shortly after seven, we began to look for blood tracks in earnest. In a little while I was heartened to find a few drops where the panther had entered the lantana, and then quite a considerable amount at a spot about forty yards inside the undergrowth. It was now quite evident that he had been badly hit and had lain down here; also that it was he who had growled so loudly the previous night, when Cedric had jumped down from the tree. In fact one realised that the panther had not driven home a charge at the time and caught us napping.

'Cedric photographed the spot. He is one of those camera-enthusiasts who take photos of practically anything and everything.

'I found that from this point a blood trail was visible for upwards of another hundred yards. Within this distance he had lain down once more, which confirmed the fact that he had been badly hit. Then the blood trail became less distinct, probaly because fat, or a piece of membrane, had covered the bullet hole and stopped the external bleeding.

'The undergrowth was fairly dense and we searched carefully everywhere, but there was no panther to be found. The forest line continued, and I walked along the edge of it, peering into the lantana in the hope of seeing the beast.

'I had gone perhaps another hundred yards, Cedric following with his camera at about twenty paces, keeping to the open of the forest line, when it suddenly happened. Evidently the panther had been lying concealed beneath a bush on the opposite side of the clearing and had escaped my notice. He waited till I had passed and then, with a characteristic coughing grunt, he charged me. Cedric was almost level with the place where the panther had been hiding, and how it had not seen him and charged him, instead of me, is a mystery and very lucky for Cedric. Probably the panther was too busy watching me and preparing to make his surprise attack. Anyhow, he charged, but hearing that coughing grunt, I sprang around in time to see him coming. Fortunately, my bullet of the night before had smashed his right foreleg, which dragged as he came on.

'Throwing my rifle to my left shoulder—from which I shoot—I pressed the trigger and sent the bullet crashing into his throat. He lurched forward on to his chest, still snarling vigorously, and this gave me time to put in a second shot.

'Only then did I notice that Cedric was close behind, and was fairly dancing with excitement. He had been in my direct line of fire, and I might have shot him instead of the panther. But this incredible enthusiast had actually taken a photo of the charge. How Cedric had the nerve to take it, when ninety-nine men out of a hundred, completely unarmed as he was, would have turned tail and fled, beats me. It only goes to show that an enthusiasm for photography enabled him to forget everything else. He tells me he just aimed the camera and depressed the shutter mechanically, without thinking what he was doing.

'When we returned to the bungalow to tell the good news, we found that Rustam and Varghese had already come back, having sat up till about 2 a.m. The mosquitoes had by this time got the better of them, and as the tiger had not put in an appearance, Rustam and his companion had decided to call it a day, and get back to the bungalow for a nap.

'We carried the panther in by nine o'clock and had skinned him in about an hour. It proved to be quite a large male, measuring 7'8" from nose to tail.

'After an early lunch, I suggested to Rustam that we should go and see about the bull over which he had sat. I must not forget to tell you that, in the meantime, Varghese had sent out men to see what had happened to the third and fourth animals. These men returned to inform us that both were still alive.

'When we reached Rustam's *machan*, we found that the tiger had returned to its kill, probably in the early hours of the morning after Rustam had got down. Perhaps it had been watching, and had come to know that he was up there. Later when the coast was clear, it had come back for a late meal. About three-quarters of the bull had been devoured.

'Rustam was extremely disappointed, but was determined to sit up again. Then I had an inspiration. Wisely, or unwisely, I sent Varghese with one of the men to fetch our fourth bait, which had been tied on the track approaching Mudiyanoor village. It took about two hours to bring this animal, and we tethered it about thirty paces from the remains of the old kill. My hope in doing this was that the tiger might be induced to attack it, in case he hesitated to return to the old kill, which had been dead for two days and was stinking horribly. Rustam opposed this plan, because he felt that the tiger would be frightened away by finding a live bull where he had left a dead one the day before. But I felt the chance was worth taking.

'At about 5.30 p.m., the three of us, Rustam, Cedric and myself, got into the *machan*, having already arranged fresh green leaves for concealment, those of the previous night having been withered by the heat. Rustam was to have the first shot, and I would follow up. Cedric had fitted a flash bulb and reflector to his beloved camera, in the hope of securing another exciting photograph.

'With the approach of dusk myriads of insects of all kinds came from the nearby pool to make our existence a torture. But we were young and extremely keen. Rustam had long been waiting for an opportunity to shoot a tiger.

'Eight o'clock came, then nine and ten, but a little later we heard the moaning call of the tiger, as it descended a hillside beyond the pool about a mile way. About forty-five minutes passed, when a kakar gave forth its hoarse call from the denseness of the bamboos to our left. It was clear the tiger was coming, and we were all keyed up with intense excitement.

'We waited. It was much darker here than it had been at my *machan* of the night before, because of the bamboos. I whispered to Rustam to wait till the tiger either attacked the live bull or came back to its old kill, when I would use my torch to help him aim. Fortunately, the live bull was a white one, and we could see it faintly, and hear it snorting and struggling, as it tried to free its leg from the tethering rope. It was clear that the creature must have had some inkling of the approaching danger and its ultimace fate.

'There was a silence for ten minutes. Then there was a deep "Woof" and the tiger sprang on to the live bull. Rustam was trembling like an aspen with suppressed excitement, but I gripped his shoulder firmly to keep him quiet. There followed a hoarse gurgle from the bull, and a sharp snapping sound as the vertebrae of its neck cracked and the carcase thudded to earth.

'I maintained my grip on Rustam's shoulder. Another period of silence followed for almost ten minutes, before the tiger began to bite the rear of the bull in its first operations to tear out and remove the entrails.

'Still we waited, and then we heard the scratching sound made by the tearing of membrane as the tiger started to pull out the bull's intestines. I judged that by now its attention would be fully occupied by its kill; so gently releasing my grip on Rustam's shoulder, I nudged him to prepare for the shot.

'He raised his rifle, as I did mine. After about ten seconds I pressed the button of my torch. As the beam shot forth, the tiger, which had been lying on its kill sideways to us, turned around and looked up. At the same moment Rustam switched on his torch too, and in the two beams the tiger was distinctly visible as he stared back. Seconds passed, and I began to wonder whether Rustam was going to fire. Then, just as I was about to press my trigger, the roar of the double-barrelled .405/400 rent the night.

'Rustam had fired both barrels simultaneously, and the kick from the heavy weapon must have been considerable; I felt him lurch violently backwards. Nevertheless, both bullets had sped true to their mark, smashing into the tiger's neck just above the shoulder. The animal shook violently and then sank forward, just as if it was going to sleep. The tail twitched a few times and then was still. Rustam had shot his first tiger.

'We waited for another half-hour, but there was no movement from the animal; so we got down from the *machan*, still keeping the torch focused on the tiger. But it never stirred. It was evident that the tiger was dead. Upon examination, Rustam was jubilant at finding he had killed a fine male, which measured 9'4" from nose to tail-tip.

'And so we returned to Bangalore, an extremely happy party. Rustam had got his tiger, and I had succeeded in killing the panther that had been harassing Mr. Hailstone's animals. But of the three of us I think Cedric Bone was the happiest at having taken a marvellously lucky photograph and a marvellously lucky escape from what would have been a severe mauling, if not a painful death, had the panther attacked him instead of me.

'I told Dad the story, and he congratulated both of us. But he never at that time realised the narrowness of Cedric's escape from the panther, as well as from my rifle bullet.

'Next day, when he saw the photograph, he started to say a lot of uncomplimentary things. At the time I felt he was rather harsh and quite unreasonable; but, as I think of it now, the old man was right.

'I had made two major mistakes. Firstly, I had not looked carefully enough in the undergrowth, and had passed the panther without seeing it. Secondly in my excitement I had fired with a human being directly in my line of fire, and about twenty paces away. They say fortune favours the beginner, and it certainly was so in this case.'

Eight

The Mauler of Rajnagara

AT THE MOMENT OF TELLING THIS STORY (NOVEMBER 1995), THE 'mauler' is still alive, having defeated every effort I made to 'bag' him. And not only my own efforts, but those of several other hunters over a period of rather more than two years.

The mauler is altogether an unusual tiger, in that his habits are very un-tigerish and his haunts are in areas where no tiger has been heard of for many years. His habits are untigerish in that the earlier records of his activities were entirely confined to mauling men by scratching them with his forefeet. There were thirty-three instances of such attacks by this tiger, his victims being mainly herdsmen. In not a single case did he either bite or kill his victim. In every case he severely scratched the man from the crown of his head, down his face and neck, and across his chest and back.

This conduct at first led me to think that the so-called tiger was really a 'panther' after all. But when at a later stage

I questioned several of his victims, every one of them affirmed that it was a tiger and not a panther that had attacked him.

I was also led to think that the animal had been wounded or otherwise injured in some part of its jaw, mouth, or face, so that he could not drive home his attack by biting his victim. This theory was entirely refuted by the herdsmen, who stated that during two years, the same tiger had killed and eaten over two hundred of their cattle. They had examined many of these kills after the event, and in no case was any evidence found that the tiger had been unable to use his teeth properly. He had not only killed his prey in regular tiger fashion by breaking its neck, but had eaten each animal in a very normal and thorough manner.

The next strange thing about this animal was that he had begun his depredations in a most un-tigerish stretch of the forest, consisting of low scrub and thorn: very rocky, undulating hillocks with occasional steep boulder-strewn rivulets between them, flanked by long grass and occasional clumps of bamboo. It was known that panthers frequently roamed this area, and had even been seen on the main road that ran through it; but a tiger was unknown to the existing generation.

This stretch of forest lies immediately to the south of the Dimbum escarpment in the district of North Coimbatore. A sharp drop of over 2,500 feet from Dimbum brings you to this region of arid scrub land, dotted with frequent palm trees, and consisting mostly of thorny bushes and lantana shrub. Other game is also scarce, being confined to a few peafowl and an occasional jungle sheep. The area is comparatively small, being about five miles from north to south, and about thirty miles from east to west, where it adjoins the Bhavani river, which eventually flows into the river Cauvery.

We are told that this tiger had originally come from the Nilgiri jungles, had wandered down to the Moyar river and then taken its abode in this region. Its fondness for this locality can otherwise be well understood, for it is an area scattered with small cattle-*patties,* and entirely devoted to grazing hundreds of cattle. Hence, what it lacks in natural wild game is more than balanced by the large number of domestic animals, which are much easier prey to any tiger.

The story goes that at the earlier stages the tiger killed normally, ate his kills normally, and decamped normally, when he was 'shooed' off his kills by enraged herdsmen. But, as the old proverb says, 'too much of anything is good for nothing'! Or, at least, this tiger seemed to think so. The herdsmen evidently made themselves too much of a nuisance to him, when too frequently they drove him off his kills.

The first attack, as is usually the case, was made on a herdsboy who had had the temerity to throw a stone at him, just as he was in the act of dragging away a fine fat cow he had killed. The stone is reported to have struck the tiger's flank; the tiger is reported to have dropped the cow and charged the boy, whom he severely scratched about the face and chest. Then he went back and carried off the cow, which he thereafter ate in peace.

On several later occasions herdsmen and boys tried to drive him off the beasts he had killed, or was in the act of carrying off, or was actually eating. In each case the tiger attacked and scratched the intruder.

Naturally, as such attacks multiplied, he was left more and more alone. He was evidently a very wise tiger and had arrived at the sensible conclusion that it paid him high dividends to scratch but not to kill the intruders; for they thereafter left him more and more to devour his kill untroubled.

And so time dragged on. Nearly two years had passed and the victims of his scratching rose to thirty-three. Of these eleven died of subsequent blood poisoning, arising from the putrid matter in the tiger's claws. But these deaths, of course, may not be regarded as intentionally caused by the tiger himself. They were only an indirect consequence of the attack.

And then, in July 1955, the first human being failed to return. It was known that he had been attacked by the tiger, for his screams for help had conveyed this information to another herdsman, who had been standing near. This individual, very naturally, had run away. In the earlier instances, the victims had generally managed to stagger back to the main road or to the cattle village, whichever happened to be nearer. But this victim did not return. Some two hours later a search party set out to look for him. They came to the spot where the attack had been made. This time they found the dead cow, but they did not find the herdsman. The party lacked the courage to follow up any further, and the herdsman was never seen again.

A half-dozen more attacks were made, in three of which the victims turned up as usual, badly scratched. But the remaining three did not. Nor were they ever seen again. So the official score, at the time my story really starts, amounted to four killings and thirty-six maulings; the mauling, in every case, only by scratching. Whether the tiger actually ate these four men it had presumably killed, or only dragged them off to some remote part of the jungle, where they had been later devoured by jackals, hyaenas and vultures, there was no means of knowing.

I had read, now and then in the papers, of this animal's doings but had no details until an official report reached me from the forest authorities. Also at about this time I had a few days' leave to my credit and thought it would be best spent in seeing if I could catch up with this tiger.

The forest map I possessed, together with the information received, indicated that the best place at which to make my headquarters would be the small village of Rajnagara, where there was a little forest 'choultry' that would give me and my belongings shelter. This place, via Dimbum, is exactly 147 miles from Bangalore, and the road being quite good, I reached it in my Studebaker in just over four hours time, at about four in the evening.

I had no idea that an exciting time was ahead of me, for I was only two miles from Rajnagara itself, and was driving along the road through the arid scrub area, when I saw three men in front of me, one of them being supported by the other two. As I drew abreast of them, I saw that the man in the middle was covered with blood. Stopping to enquire the reason, I was told that only a few minutes earlier he had been attacked and severely scratched by this strange tiger. Closer questioning elicited the fact that the tiger had attacked him after creeping up on him by stealth. The victim told me that, before he knew he was in any danger, he had heard a low growl; then the tiger appeared beside him, reared up on its hind feet and scratched him severely about his face and chest. He had fallen down with the tiger on top of him, and had shouted for help. The tiger then left him and charged the cattle, which were milling around. As he lay bleeding on the ground, he had seen the tiger kill a half-grown brown bullock, which it had then dragged away. As nobody had come to his assistance, he had struggled to his feet and stumbled towards the road, still shouting for help. His two companions had joined him a little later.

I regarded the opportunity as godsend, to be followed up at once, and asked him to tell his companions the exact locality where the attack had taken place. He did so, and I then asked for one of the men to accompany me to the spot, while the other went on to Rajnagara with the victim.

A heated altercation now took place between them, both pleading urgent business at the village. It was clearly apparent that neither wanted to expose himself to the risk of meeting the tiger. For this I could hardly blame them, as the animal had already established his ferocity, while I was a complete stranger to them. They had absolutely no guarantee that I would not run away when the tiger showed up, and leave my companion in its clutches.

By much pleading, coercion and even threats, I eventually induced one of the men, very reluctantly, to agree to come with me, while the other continued with the wounded man.

My companion and myself then left the road and walked into the jungle. All along the *path* we came on splashes of blood from the recently wounded man. In crossing a bare stretch of rock these were plentiful, causing me to realise that he had been more severely hurt than I had actually noticed during my hurried conversation. I began to think that I should have taken him in my car to Satyamangalam, where there was a hospital, rather than leave the poor fellow to get there as best he could. Against this admitted negligence on my part, however, was the fact that I had a unique opportunity to meet this tiger face to face and settle the score once and for all.

A little later we came to the spot where the tiger had attacked the man. The sand on the trail clearly told its own story. We began to look around for the place where the tiger had killed the brown bullock, and soon found it some thirty yards away. My companion now refused to go any further, nor did I want him to, as he was understandably in a state of abject fear and would be much more a liability than an asset. So I left him standing nervously and began to follow the dragmark clearly made by the tiger as he had hauled the brown bull downhill towards the ravine that lay between the hillock down which I was creeping, and another and much higher hillock a quarter of a mile away.

THE MAULER OF RAJNAGARA

Unfortunately, I had not anticipated such early action, and was wearing ordinary leather shoes instead of the rubber-soled boots I favoured for stalking. Try as I would, these shoes made some noise on the hard ground and the rocky boulders that were scattered there. Nevertheless I proceeded as silently as I could, till I had almost reached the *nullah*. Then I stopped and gazed about me. The scrub just here was very thick, and grew thicker where the rivulet was actually winding. My eyes roved over the slopes of the opposite hillock, which were fairly open. No signs of the tiger or the bullock were visible, and it was obvious that he must have hidden it somewhere in the *nullah,* and most probably would be eating it at that very moment. Even if he was not actually eating it, he would certainly be lying somewhere in the vicinity.

My shoes put me at a distinct disadvantage, and would betray my further progress towards that *nullah*. If I removed them and attempted to advance in my stockinged feet, I was almost certain to step on a thorn, not to speak of the sharp stones that lay everywhere. At the same time, I realised the opportunity was too good to be lost, and should be pressed home somehow. It was a chance in a thousand, which I might never get again. The time was just 5 p.m., and there was an hour and a half before sunset.

While I stood debating the odds, the tiger made the first move. He had quite obviously heard me; probably he had seen me too. Anyhow he had, after the manner of a great general, decided to make a flank attack. Quite unsuspected by me, he had already crept up the very slope down which I was moving, but at a slightly different angle, which brought him above and behind the spot where I stood thinking. Then he had evidently crept on his belly towards me, and was hiding behind a large bush, scarcely ten feet away, all unknown to me. In this particular case, my sixth sense of impending peril quite failed to register. I had just decided to advance towards the *nullah*, when there was a shattering roar behind me, and the tiger sprang out; I spun around and fired at point-blank range, missing him completely.

Probably the noise of the explosion, perhaps the strangeness of meeting someone who was obviously not a herdsman, or maybe rather the loud scarlet-and-blue check bush-coat I happened to be wearing, scared him off. For with a series of loud *'Woofs'* he bounded into the thicket and towards the *nullah*. I followed as fast as I could, reaching the bed of the *nullah*, where I almost fell over the brown bull. Examination showed that the tiger had already begun his meal before he had heard or sensed my approach, and had come forward on his own to the attack.

There were no trees in the vicinity, so I sat under the thick bush till it began to grow dark, hoping against hope that the tiger might put in a second appearance. But this he did not do, and at 6.15 I cautiously retraced my steps the way I had come. Reaching the place where I left the herdsman who had accompanied me, I found him missing and concluded he had gone home. So I went on to the road where my Studebaker stood, and shortly after reached Rajnagara.

Here a considerable crowd had gathered, and from a forest guard who was among them I found that the wounded herdsman had already proceeded to Satyamangalam hospital, together with his wife and brother. The herdsman who had accompanied me, whom I had left standing at the spot where the tiger had made his attack, while I had followed up the drag-mark alone, had failed to return.

I knew that he had not been at the place where I had left him, also that the tiger had run away after I had missed it. Where had the herdsman gone? We all realised that he would not remain in the jungle, or on the road, in a vicinity haunted by this tiger. What had become of him? I pondered this question, while his wife and family, who were also among the crowd and had overheard my enquiries, began to weep and wail.

It was now quite dark, and to search for the missing man would be impossible, as no traces would be visible had the tiger taken him away. Nevertheless, calling the forest guard to accompany me, I drove back to the spot where I had earlier left the car. Here we halted for a while, and I instructed the guard to call the man by name. This produced no results. We drove a further mile along the road and then returned to the village. By now it was evident to me that my companion of the evening before had been taken by the tiger. Evidently, while I had spent an hour sitting in the *nullah*, watching for the tiger to return to the carcase of the brown bull, the tiger had done some hunting on his own, and had carried off the unfortunate herdsman.

We did not get much sleep that night, having to listen to the weeping and wailing of the man's family, who squatted at the door of the forest choultry and amidst tears, reminded me that I was responsible for his death. This though impinged itself on my conscience very forcibly, for had I not almost forced the poor man to accompany me he would have been alive at that moment.

Early dawn found me retracing my steps to the spot where I had left him. Reaching it, I began looking around for any signs of struggle or other marks of the tiger's attack. Absolutely nothing was visible on the hard ground.

In the course of my search I walked around in ever widening circles, but still could find nothing. What had become of him was a mystery. I knew he had not followed me while I had pursued the tiger the previous evening. It was more likely that, being afraid of standing alone, he had begun to walk back towards the road. Working on this theory, I now turned back and slowly retraced my steps, looking around for possible traces.

About three hundred yards from where I had left him I found the first evidence in the form of an odd leather sandal, and not far away its fellow. At this spot short dry grass covered the ground and so no footprints were visible. But the position of the sandals made it clear to me that he had kicked them off, obviously in order to run faster. Searching around as I walked, I then saw something white flapping in the breeze under a bush to my left. It was the man's *loincloth* in India known as a '*dhoti*'. On the grass, and sprinkled on the bushes, were tiny splashes of blood, while closer inspection showed where the tiger had dashed through the undergrowth and caught up with its victim. From here the tiger had dragged the man in a course almost parallel with the road, towards the same *nullah* in which I had been sitting all the while the evening before, but considerably further down from where he had hidden the brown bull.

I must have walked a quarter of a mile before eventually stepping on to the rocky bed of this rivulet. Nothing was to be seen and here was complete silence. I knew the tiger must have hidden the remains somewhere in the vicinity.

While watching quietly, a couple of magpies attracted my attention from a spot about one hundred yards downstream. They were perched on the top of a thorny *babul* tree, where they were jabbering excitedly, frequently looking downward. The signs of the jungle are very clear to those who can read them. The magpies had either found the body, or were looking at the tiger, who in turn was probably looking at me.

Keeping to the centre of the *nullah*, I began to tiptoe forward, the rubber boots I was wearing this time making no noise against the rocks. Halfway to the *babul* tree, the magpies saw me, ceased their jabbering and flew off.

THE MAULER OF RAJNAGARA

I had marked the spot where they had been perched, and approached cautiously. Immediately below the *babul* tree, a small elongated black rock jutted from the bank on to the bed of the stream, and lying behind this rock were the half-eaten remains of poor Muniappa, the missing man. Soft sand at the spot also revealed the tiger's pug-marks, and a cursory examination of them showed that the animal was a male tiger of no great size or build.

Once again, there was no tree in the vicinity on which I could sit, except the aforementioned *babul,* which was unusable because of its thorny nature. Nor, as it happened, were there any large bushes or bamboo clumps under which I could shelter. In every way the spot was about the most unfavourable, if not impossible, one for 'sitting up' that I had ever encountered. Still, I would have to do something about it for by this time there was absolutely no doubt in my mind that I was, at least indirectly, possibly directly, the cause of poor Muniappa's death.

I knew the tiger was not likely to return to his meal until the afternoon at the earliest. If I left the body as it was, the vultures would see it within a couple of hours and pick it clean. So I removed the khaki coat I was wearing and spread it over the corpse, weighing it down here and there with small boulders that lay at hand. Then I went back to the car and returned to Rajnagara.

Here I was forced to give the bad news, which not only led to renewed wailing, but a demand from the bereaved wife that the body of her husband be brought back at once for cremation. It took us a full hour to persuade her to give me a chance, that evening, for a shot at the tiger by sitting over the body, a chance which would be entirely lost if she had her way. Eventually, she very grudgingly assented.

After breakfast, I called a 'Council of War', which consisted of the village *Patel*, the forest guard and myself. Explaining to them the position in which I had left the body, I told them that I would return to it at noon and sit beside the body to wait the tiger's return. They thought this was a foolish idea, and I heartily concurred. But as nobody could suggest a better one, there was no alternative but to carry it out, other than to bring the remains back to the village and thereby lose a possible shot at the tiger.

Shortly after midday found me seated a few yards from the cadaver, from which a distinctly unpleasant odour was now rising. In fact, millions of bluebottles had already settled on my coat, and as soon as I removed it they swarmed over the remains.

I was prepared for the unpleasant situation, having plugged small wads of cotton wool into my nostrils; but despite these measures that awful stench penetrated my defences, and in time I began to feel sick. The heat was terrible. The silence was absolute, except for the chirruping of the cicadas from the branches of the surrounding bushes.

Three o'clock passed, then four and then five. At five-thirty a peacock flapped down to the streambed. As I sat motionless he had not even noticed me, which goes to confirm how invaluable absolute stillness is when out in a forest. He walked up the bed and only when ten feet away did he become aware of the two strange objects before him. He rose into the air, hurriedly and heavily, with a tremendous beating of his wings to gain momentum before he was able to fly away.

As may be imagined, I was by this time in a state of great excitement, and even greater fear, and I was, besides, on the verge of retching from the awful stench that rose from the half-eaten man.

Then followed complete silence for fifteen minutes: a silence that was all-pervading, that envelops one, that is everywhere, even in the very air. There was not even the creak of the wood-cricket, nor the twitter of the tiniest bird, nor even the faintest rustle of a dry leaf falling to the ground. Only a total and absolute stillness. That is what silence feels like, when one sits waiting for a man-eater to appear.

Although I was sitting perfectly motionless, my eyes minutely searched the scrub before me and on either side. All my senses were fully and painfully alert. But no sight nor sound registered on them.

The cheery evening crow of a junglecock, a little further up the *nullah*, relieved the tension. Six o'clock came, and then six-fifteen. An early nightjar began his peculiar clucking call. I knew that the time had come for me to leave. In a short while it would be completely dark, and then to sit for the man-eater in the open would be suicide indeed.

Getting stiffly to my feet, I walked back to the car, where I had previously arranged for a party of men to meet me and bring back the remains of the unfortunate Muniappa. It was quite dark by the time I collected them. But I knew my torchlight and their numbers would render us immune from any attack by the tiger. We returned to the ravine, where we gathered up all that remained of the unlucky herdsman in an old blanket which the men had brought with them for the purpose. Then, while the little procession wended its way towards Rajnagara, I motored back along the road.

Early next day found me again prowling about near the little *nullah*. The tiger had not returned to the spot where the body had been, as I could see by the absence of tracks. I then decided to walk along the bed of this stream towards the place where the brown bull had been left two days previously. I did this very cautiously, as the stream bed narrowed in places to hardly more than six feet and at points was nothing more than a pile of boulders or was entirely overgrown with lantana shrub. The brown bull had been hidden more than half a mile from where the man had been eaten. It had been hidden well beneath an overhanging bush I knew was safe from vultures. But when I reached it, it was only to find that the tiger had returned during the night and demolished it completely. Perhaps he had lost interest in his human kill or may have seen me earlier in the evening, sitting beside it, and become suspicious. Anyhow, the fact was that no kill remained and I would have to try other means of meeting the tiger.

Up till noon that day, and again in the evening I roamed about over hillocks and through valleys, across other streams and along their beds. Many times I came across the tracks of the tiger, but never once did I see him, nor catch any sign of his presence in the vicinity.

I spent three days in this fashion, but with entirely negative results. I had taken only a week's leave and had scarcely four days left in which to shoot the tiger.

Next morning I adopted fresh tactics. Climbing to the top of a large hillock in the centre of the terrain, I called as loudly as possible, in tiger fashion. Every ten minutes or so I repeated the call, hoping to hear an answer. Two hours later I did the same thing on a neighbouring hill. No sound came in reply. In the evening I followed the same plan, and yet the tiger did not respond. It was clear by this time that he was not in the immediate vicinity.

On the fifth day the herdsmen went out again with their cattle. You, who read this, may consider it a very brave thing on their part, and doubtless it was. But you must also realise the cattle were dependent for their food entirely on grazing. No grazing meant no food, for no provision had been made in any of the cattle villages for a reserve of fodder.

That morning, I joined the herdsmen and wandered amongst their animals, doing the same thing in the evening.

But night fell without any sign of the tiger. The sixth morning found me very despondent, as I felt the animal I was after had moved away and would not give me a second chance to bag him. But there was nothing more I could do, beyond mixing with the various herds of cattle as they grazed in the area.

I covered a number of miles that morning and was about eight miles from the place where Muniappa had been killed when, at about noon a group of men came running through the shrub to tell me that another herdsman had been attacked three miles away.

I hurried with them to where the man was lying. I saw once more the familiar signs: severe scratches across face, chest and sides, but no bite whatever. This man had lost a good deal of blood and was too weak to walk, so I hurried back to my car, instructing the men to carry him to the road. From there I took him to Satyamangalam, where I left him in the local hospital in pretty bad shape. Then I dashed back to the spot on the road to which he had been carried, left the car and went back into the jungle. There was no difficulty in following the copious blood trail he had left behind him, and this led me to the site of the attack.

In this case I discovered that the tiger had not succeeded in killing any of the cattle, which had escaped by stampeding *en masse* to the road. So searching for the tiger seemed again a hopeless undertaking. I wandered around, and every now and again called in tiger fashion, hoping to attract him. There was no response, and so ended another day.

That night I thought of motoring up and down the road that led through the shrub for about five miles, using my spotlight in the hope of picking up the tiger's eyes, should he be passing anywhere within range. I began to put this plan into practice at about 10 p.m., driving slowly, allowing for a stop of fifteen minutes at the end of each trip. Six hours of this monotonous procedure found me desperately sleepy and with a very low petrol tank.

Thus dawned the seventh and last day of my leave. After the latest attack, the herdsmen had not turned out with their cattle, so for the last time I wandered alone through the scrub, hoping to meet the elusive tiger. Noon found me about six miles from my car, when I turned and began to retrace steps.

I was walking down hillock and just reached the small depression at the foot of it. Before me another hillock rose. No stream traversed this valley, which was dotted with a few stunted *babul* trees, growing amidst the usual lantana and other shrubs. Hardly fifty yards ahead, the tiger stalked out. We saw each other at the same moment, and then, with a short bound, he disappeared behind a lantana clump.

Raising the rifle to my shoulder I advanced slowly, expecting, and even hoping, for a charge that would bring him to my sights. At the same time I was mortally afraid, and my heart beat a loud tattoo.

The charge never came! A sixth sense appeared to have told him that here was no victim, but one who was deliberately out to destroy him. He must have slipped away before I drew level with the bush behind which he had disappeared, for he most certainly was not there. I walked around it and searched everywhere, but I never saw him again.

Thus ended my seventh and last day. The time had now come for me to return to Bangalore and duty.

Although this is the story of an unsuccessful hunt—indeed, a story of complete failure—I have told it so that the reader may realise that such adventures are not always crowned with success. Failure and disappointment are far more frequent. But the hard work, strenuous effort, the very thrill of the chase, the pitting of human brains against animal instinct—

all these factors are there, and to a considerable extent compensate the enthusiast for his failure. For although I was really sorry that I had to leave the herdsmen, at least for some time, to the continued ravages of this animal, I felt satisfied that I had done my best and I looked forward to returning, when I might meet with better luck.

I handed a cheque to Muniappa's widow and started on that five-mile stretch of road on the beginning of my return journey to Bangalore. As the thorn bushes flashed past the car, I bade a temporary farewell to that extremely cunning and quite extraordinary tiger, which had not only succeeded in outwitting me at every encounter, but had also successfully hidden the reason for his peculiar habit of only scratching and not biting his victims—except those he actually killed.